GARDEN SECRETS FOR
ATTRACTING BIRDS

SECOND EDITION

Garden Secrets for Attracting Birds, Second Edition was produced for
Creative Homeowner by Moseley Road Inc.
129 Main Street, Irvington, NY 10533
www.moseleyroad.com

Garden Secrets for Attracting Birds, Second Edition (2021) is a revised edition of Garden Secrets for Attracting Birds (2010), published by Creative Homeowner. Revisions include new photographs and a new gallery.

MOSELEY ROAD INC.

EDITORIAL DIRECTOR	Lisa Purcell
ART DIRECTOR	Brian MacMullen
DESIGN AND LAYOUT	Terasa Bernard, Amy Pierce, Hwaim Holly Lee
EDITORS	Tricia Wright, Lori Baird
PHOTO COORDINATOR	Terasa Bernard
CONTRIBUTING WRITERS	Jon Derengowski, Lisa Purcell
COVER DESIGNER	Gus Yoo
CARTOGRAPHER	Neil Dvorak

ISBN 978-1-58011-863-7

Library of Congress Control Number: 2020944575

We are always looking for talented authors. To submit an idea, please send a brief inquiry to acquisitions@foxchapelpublishing.com.

Printed in Singapore

Current Printing (last digit)
10 9 8 7 6 5 4 3 2 1

CREATIVE HOMEOWNER®
www.creativehomeowner.com

Creative Homeowner books are distributed in North America by
Fox Chapel Publishing, 903 Square Street, Mount Joy, PA 17552, and in the
UK by Grantham Book Service, Trent Road, Grantham, Lincolnshire NG31 7XQ.

GARDEN SECRETS FOR
ATTRACTING BIRDS

A Bird-by-Bird Guide to Favored Plants

SECOND EDITION

RACHAEL LANICCI

CRE**A**TIVE
HOMEOWNER®

Contents

Birds and Gardens: A Perfect Partnership

Birds and humans have always enjoyed a happy relationship, albeit one that involves a fair bit of mystery. Birds spend a lot of their time out of reach and out of sight. Expert aviators that they are, they swoop in to take advantage of a few dropped crumbs or, more often, distract us with a pleasant song while safely ensconced inside a shrub or sitting pretty on a towering branch. It's their unbelievable diversity and mastery of the sky that inspires awe in us, and to behold a bird up close is a truly special event.

A fleeting glimpse of a single bird brings even the most ordinary landscape to life, so it's no wonder we take particular comfort in the presence of these creatures. Even in the most urban settings, seemingly devoid of so much as a single bough, you can attract and even cater to visiting birds with the proper care and planning. A yard or garden needn't be enormous, as long as it offers the things birds need and love.

What Birds Like

Birds' basic requirements aren't so different from our own—they need food, water, and shelter. Birds will ignore places without these things and quickly grow fond of locations that provide all three.

Density and variety are the keys to planning a garden that birds will love—and perhaps even come to call home. Different species of trees, shrubs, flowers, and plants attract specific birds; the more variety your garden has, the more likely you are to spot an interesting or rare bird up close.

An American Goldfinch rests in a patch of purple coneflower.

Birds need open space in which to feed and fly, but they also need places to hide and rest. By "layering" your garden with plants of different sizes, you'll encourage birds to do both right in your backyard.

How to Do It

In the city, a small combination of interesting plants, shrubs, and flowers clustered tightly together, along with a miniature birdbath and a food source, is enough to entice birds to make a stop on your balcony, porch, or windowsill. If you're fortunate enough to have a courtyard or a flat rooftop deck, the placement of more permanent greenery, such as potted trees and flower beds, will make the area that much more attractive to birds.

Rural and suburban areas have even more potential for bird hospitality. The average yard, with its mown lawn and dearth of trees, offers little enticement to our feathered friends. If your garden is just starting out, plant in stages to maximize variety and allow for future growth and maturity. Combine different kinds of trees (coniferous and deciduous), flowers (annuals and perennials), and other plant life to attract the maximum number and variety of bird species. There's no magic combination, and you needn't establish a Garden of Eden overnight—the birds will be grateful for any effort you make.

What You'll Learn

Depending on the region in which you live, some species of flowers and plants work better than others. This book gives you planting, growing, and habit information for particular species that thrive in various North American climates, as well as the specific birds that are attracted to them.

North America is home to a terrific variety of bird species. Once you've attracted the birds to your garden, you'll want to know what they are. Use the guide starting on page 42 to identify the birds you see and hear, based on their distinct appearance, song, and call. Come across eggs or a nest? Don't disturb them, but try to determine the species to which they might belong.

Feeling at Home: Birdhouses, Birdbaths, Fountains, and Ponds

Once the basic, natural components of your garden are in place, there are a number of man-made structures that offer visiting birds additional room to hide, rest, or even nest while they incubate and raise their young. Properly constructed and placed, these structures provide birds with even more reason to linger nearby and greatly increase your chances of intimately observing their patterns and rituals.

Birdhouses

Adding a small birdhouse or two to your garden or backyard is a simple but very effective way to attract birds. A birdhouse offers a place to perch or nest and will be particularly welcome in the winter when there may be little in the way of natural shelter.

If you have the room, experiment with a variety of different-size birdhouses, varying the size of the entrance and the shape of the house in particular. Depending on the dimensions, different species will take up residence. If you plan to purchase a preconstructed birdhouse, identify a few of your favorite bird species, and find a house designed to attract them.

If you elect to take the do-it-yourself route, you can customize a birdhouse to your own specifications, taking into consideration the

climate in which you live and the birds you'd like to welcome. When building many species houses, resist the temptation to include a protruding ledge or perch outside the entrance—this provides an easy way for predators, such as squirrels, to enter the house. Most birds are perfectly happy to perch on the entrance hole itself. Many birdhouses can be constructed at home with only minimal supplies and skills, and you may enjoy the project as much as you do gardening!

A weathered birdhouse

Nesting Shelves, Boxes, and Baskets

A nesting shelf is a simple, sturdy piece of wood placed in a tree or against a wall to provide birds with a secure platform on which to build their nest when the time comes. Birds such as robins and phoebes, which do not like to be confined, prefer a nesting shelf to a house. Nesting boxes provide a bit more cover.

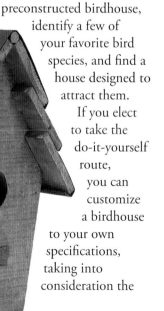

A homemade birdhouse

BUILDING YOUR OWN BIRDHOUSE

- Select clean, untreated wood—rough-hewn pieces will give the birds some traction.
- Ensure that your design includes a roof with an inch or two of overhang to keep the house dry.
- Incorporate hinges or screws for easy disassembly and seasonal cleaning.
- Provide holes at the top and bottom for ventilation and drainage.
- Make sure that the main entrance is near the top of the house.
- If you paint the house, select only nontoxic paint in natural colors, and never paint the inside.
- Install the house in a secluded location away from other birdhouses—nesting birds can be territorial.

A few of the tenants take the air at a Purple Martin "apartment complex."

Bluebird House

In the mid-1990s, the disappearing habitat of the Eastern Bluebird meant that this North American thrush faced extinction. Thanks to a network of bird lovers who erected nesting boxes, the numbers of this vibrant-colored species are back on the rise. You, too, can attract these lovely birds to your backyard by setting up a nesting box, which comes in a specific shape and a few sizes. Bluebirds will begin to nest as early as March and, unlike the sociable Purple Martin, they prefer their houses to be spaced well apart.

The decaying or dead trunk of a tree makes an attractive nest site for many species, some of which actually excavate a hole first.

For the best results, birdhouses and boxes should be made from simple, natural materials and located in positions that afford the birds some amount of privacy and protection. Try to position birdhouses so that their entrances don't face the wind.

A nest basket is another simple kind of bird house that you can easily build and hang in your backyard to attract mating pairs of birds, such as Mourning Doves. Many birds are opportunists when it comes to choosing nesting sites, and you may find nests in the hollows of cactuses, in the branches of shrubbery, and even in the hanging flower baskets swinging from your porch and inside the potted plants on your deck. Never disturb your baskets and pots after you notice eggs—the parents will likely abandon the nest if it's moved.

Purple Martin Apartment

Purple Martins, especially those in eastern North America, rely on nest boxes to breed, and many of them roost in colonies. Set up a martin "apartment complex," with many pegs, perches, and entrance holes in a desirable location, and your "tenants" will return year after year.

A pair of Eastern Bluebirds take advantage of a ready-made home.

A curious American Robin surveys the company at a lawn birdbath.

THE BEST BIRDBATH

- The water in a birdbath should be very shallow—no more than 3 inches deep.
- Choose (or build) a birdbath with a rough surface on the bottom and edges.
- Arrange a few stones or other elements in the middle of the basin to provide landing space.
- Place your birdbath in a clearing—birds like to have advance warning of predators.
- Keep the birdbath and surrounding area clean.
- Change the water every few days.

Birdbaths, Fountains, and Ponds

Installing a birdbath in your garden is an excellent way to encourage a variety of species to drop by for an invigorating splash. Many backyard birds enjoy taking a bath in a pond or birdbath, and on a warm summer day, few birds will pass up a cool sip from an inviting source of water. These need not be limited to traditional stone lawn monuments, but can also feature a bubbling fountain or include a heating element for freezing weather. Many birds are attracted to the sound of moving water, particularly those that enjoy perching by a stream. To create a genuine bird sanctuary in your garden, consider installing a small pond edged with rocks and fitted with a pump, which will simulate the irresistible sounds of a stream. A simpler and less expensive option is to make a very small hole in a large drum or jug, and suspend it over your birdbath. Fill it with water, and the dripping sound will ensure every bird in the area notices the new bathing site.

A small garden pond, planted with a variety of plant species, will attract plenty of feathered visitors.

Bird Feeders:
An Invitation to Dine

Providing a safe and steady source of food will encourage birds to return to your garden again and again. You will not only attract more birds but also contribute to their health by providing them with nutrients they may have difficulty finding on their own—above and beyond what they've already gleaned from your garden. Birds' nutrition is particularly crucial in the winter months, when a well-stocked feeder will supply birds with the nutrition that they will need to survive in the coldest climates. The kind of bird feeder that you choose is ultimately a matter of preference: some of them withstand the elements better than others; some attract different types of birds; and some work well in certain environments where others do not. You might find that a combination of different bird feeders will best suit your needs.

Tubular Feeder

A tubular bird feeder is a long, narrow cylinder, commonly made of plastic, which is filled with a seed mixture and hung from a tree branch or other similar support. The cylinders are fitted with perches and punctured with small holes that allow the birds to reach the seeds. The length of the perch determines the types of birds that will come to a tubular feeder—larger birds will come to longer perches and smaller birds to shorter perches. To deter squirrels—notorious for raiding bird feeders—many tubular feeders come encased in a metal cage; this allows birds to feed but keeps out unwelcome visitors.

Niger Feeder

Niger, also called niger thistle, is a tall yellow flower of the sunflower family that produces tiny, oil-rich seeds that many birds love. A niger feeder is designed for storing these smaller seeds and is a suitable choice for attracting sparrows, chickadees, titmice, grosbeaks, and many finch species, especially goldfinches. This bird feeder is often similar

Pine Siskins gather to feast on the offerings at a tubular feeder.

11

A Black-capped Chickadee makes a dinner stop at a niger stocking feeder.

to a regular tubular feeder, but it is made smaller and narrower to accommodate the tiny seeds. In place of the small holes on a tubular bird feeder, niger feeders usually include small openings with spill trays, which provide easy access to the seeds. A niger stocking feeder offers another way to give birds what they crave. This feeder dispenses seeds from a netted cloth stocking, usually made of nylon or vinyl.

Suet Feeder

A suet bird feeder is a wire or nylon mesh bag containing a block or cake of suet. Suet is a calorie-dense, fatty mixture composed of rendered animal fat mixed with seeds, nuts, and fruit in any combination, usually sold in preformed blocks that can be inserted into a suet feeder. You can also easily make your own

Hungry sparrows aren't shy about getting their share at a suet feeder.

suet balls. Typically, suet is made from beef fat, but it is also available in insect- or vegetable-based varieties. Suet is a great source of nutrition for birds in the winter months, when protein is scarce. A suet bird

A pair of Mourning Doves dine at a tray feeder.

female Ruby-throated Hummingbird makes a stop to sip sugar water at a hummingbird feeder.

eeder is suitable for a wide range of birds, including woodpeckers, goldfinches, juncos, cardinals, thrushes, ys, kinglets, tits, bluebirds, and wrens.

Platform/Tray Feeder

his simple bird feeder is a tray onto which food is irectly placed, and it is particularly suited to juncos, oves, and sparrows. Although sometimes covered by a oof, this bird feeder is very open, offering little protec- ion from scavenging squirrels or inclement weather. To educe rain-induced sogginess and damage, make sure hat your platform feeder has adequate drainage. As you night expect, this type of bird feeder is best suited to a ry environment.

Northern Cardinal samples the seed selection at a hopper feeder.

FEEDING THE MASSES

Sunflower seeds are generally a flock-pleaser. Of the two kinds—black-oil and striped—striped are harder for house sparrows and blackbirds to crack open. If you see more of these birds than you'd like, striped sunflower seeds may be preferable.

Shelled sunflower seeds are a good option if you'd rather not clean up shells, but they're more expensive, and they attract squirrels and predators. They also tend to spoil if left in a feeder for too long.

Hopper Feeder

A hopper feeder is similar to a platform feeder, but its walls offer greater protection against the elements. The more enclosed design of this bird feeder also encourages the growth of mold, so a good drainage system is a must. It is equally important to clean the hopper feeder and change the food regularly. A squirrel-proof version of this bird feeder is designed with a weighted perch that will shut off access to the food if anything heavier than a bird rests on it. The hopper feeder will attract most species of birds.

Hummingbird Feeder

This is a unique type of bird feeder that dispenses a sugary water solution to hungry hummingbirds and other nectar-loving birds. Usually made of plastic, this feeder has small holes or protruding spouts into which a hummingbird can insert its beak and reach the solution inside. Typically, this bird feeder will have a red hood or base to imitate the red flowers that hummingbirds find so appealing. Under no circumstances should you add red dye to your solution, however, because the dye is potentially harmful to birds. To make your own nectar, add one-half cup of granulated sugar to two cups of boiling water, and stir until the sugar is fully dissolved. (Let the solution cool before filling your feeder.) The rule of thumb to remember in making nectar is a 4:1 ratio of water to sugar.

A Baltimore Oriole satisfies his sweet tooth at an oriole fruit feeder.

Oriole Fruit Feeder

Provide orioles with nourishment during their breeding season by putting out an oriole bird feeder, which dispenses nectar, jelly, and/or fruit, rather than seeds. Many oriole feeders look like orange hummingbird feeders, and like the hummingbird variety, they dispense a sugar-water solution that simulates flower nectar. There are also feeders constructed to dispense jelly or jam or to hold oranges, which orioles love.

Buy the Best Seed

Birds are notoriously picky creatures, and what they choose to eat is no exception. Seed provides birds with well-rounded nutrition, in addition to the insects and plants they'll find in your garden, and as is the case with nests and houses, certain species have certain preferences.

CHOOSING THE RIGHT MIX

There are many kinds of seeds, and each attracts many kinds of birds. Here is a rundown of the major kinds.

- **SAFFLOWER**
  Attracts: Cardinals, chickadees, doves, finches, grosbeaks, nuthatches, sparrows, and titmice
  Best feeders: Hopper; tray

- **WHITE MILLET**
  Attracts: Sparrows, doves, towhees, juncos, and cardinals
  Best feeders: Ground; tray
  Avoid if you live near: Blackbirds and cowbirds
  Alternative: Black-oil sunflower

- **CRACKED CORN**
  Attracts: Cardinals, doves, grosbeaks, and jays
  Best feeder: Tray
  Avoid if you live near: House sparrows, starlings, geese, cowbirds, and squirrels and other scavengers

- **PEANUTS**
  Attracts: Chickadees, jays, titmice, and woodpeckers
  Best feeders: Tray; tube
  Avoid if you live near: Squirrels, bears, and other scavengers

- **SORGHUM**
  Attracts: Jays
  Best feeders: Ground, tray
  Avoid if you live near: Cowbirds

- **RAPESEED**
  Attracts: Doves, finches, and juncos

- **NIGER**
  Attracts: Finches, sparrows, chickadees, titmice, and grosbeaks
  Best feeder: Tube (with fine mesh)

Birds love seed, but so do many other animals you might not want in your garden, including squirrels, bears, raccoons, deer, and other scavengers. These animals already take advantage of many intentional (and unintentional) human food sources and don't need more excuses to graze.

Pay close attention to the labels on your seed—the best seed is pure and doesn't contain any additives or filler, such as flax. Fillers don't provide any nutrition to birds, and they create waste and potential contamination.

Bee Balm

Blueberry

Hosta

Sunflower

...y Spruce

Bird-Attracting Trees, Shrubs, and Plants

Eastern Redcedar

American Holly

Ilex opaca

ORDER: Aquifoliales | FAMILY: Aquifoliace:

A slow-growing evergreen, the American holly has thick, leathery leaves edged with spikelike points. This sturdy plant's thorny branches provide protection for many nesting birds and are home to a host of insects, such as bees, ants, and moths, which in turn assist in its pollination. It bears small, greenish white flowers in spring, and in the fall, it produces small red berries, which remain on the plant through the winter. The berries are poisonou to humans, but they form a staple of many songbirds' winter diets. Each berry contains four individual seeds. The evergreen foliage also provides birds with shelter from predators during the winter months, when many other trees are bare. The American holly is often associated with the Christmas holiday season.

American Redstart

Yellow-billed Cuckoo

Blue Jay

GROWING GUIDE

- **TYPE:** Evergreen shrub
- **BLOOMS:** Spring
- **LIGHT:** Partial shade
- **SOIL:** Well-drained, moist, slightly acidic
- **MOISTURE:** Moderate
- **pH:** 4–7.5
- **SPACING:** 15–40 feet
- **PLANTING:** Balled and burlapped
- **HEIGHT:** 12–60 feet
- **SPREAD:** 10–20 feet
- **HARDINESS ZONE:** 5b–9b

Bachelor's Button

Centaurea cyanus

ORDER: Asterales | FAMILY: Asteraceae

Birds love seeds, so planting flowers that form large seed heads will benefit both the bird-watching gardener and garden-visiting birds. Bachelor's button, also called cornflower, boutonniere flower, and bluebottle, is one such annual. Bachelor's button is known for the distinctive blue of its ragged-edged flowers, which after its summer bloom, produce seeds that appeal to cardinals, chickadees, finches,

nuthatches, and titmice. Its intense blue color makes it a popular garden plant, although nurseries now offer cultivars in pink, white, lavender, and a maroon so dark it appears black. Bachelor's button, ranging in height from 10 inches to 2½ feet, produces fringed blooms and attractive gray-green leaves. It is a popular cut flower, often paired in bouquets with yellow and white daisies and asters.

Tufted
Titmouse

Red-breasted
Nuthatch

Northern
Cardinal

GROWING GUIDE

- **TYPE:** Annual
- **Blooms:** Early summer to early fall
- **LIGHT:** Full sun
- **SOIL:** Well-drained; alkaline
- **MOISTURE:** Moderate
- **pH:** 6.6–7.8
- **SPACING:** 9–24 inches
- **PROPAGATION:** Seeds
- **HEIGHT:** 2–3 feet
- **SPREAD:** 12 inches
- **HARDINESS ZONE:** 2a–11

BACHELOR'S BUTTON CULTIVARS

- 'Blue' is the classic deep cornflower blue.
- 'Blue Boy' is a soft sky blue.
- 'Red Ball' is a vibrant raspberry pink.
- 'Black Magic' is a dramatic blackish maroon.
- 'Snowman' is a creamy white.

Bee Balm

Genus *Monarda*

ORDER: Lamiales | FAMILY: Lamiacea‹

Colorful, mint-scented bee balm is a hummingbird magnet. Bee balm, also called horsemint, Oswego tea, and bergamot, has a long history as a medicinal plant. Native Americans brewed the leaves of this herb into a restorative tea and as a tisane to treat stomach and bronchial ailments. The cultivated varieties of bee balm feature spiky blooms, which come in a range of colors, from snowy whites to brilliant crimsons, that attract butterflies, bees, and hummingbirds. The wild form sports wispy blossoms of a delicate lavender hue. Bee balm ranges in height from 1 to 3 feet, and its toothy, lance-shaped leaves exude a highly fragrant oil when crushed. Crumble some freshly picked bee balm leaves to add a spicy flavor to salads and summer drinks.

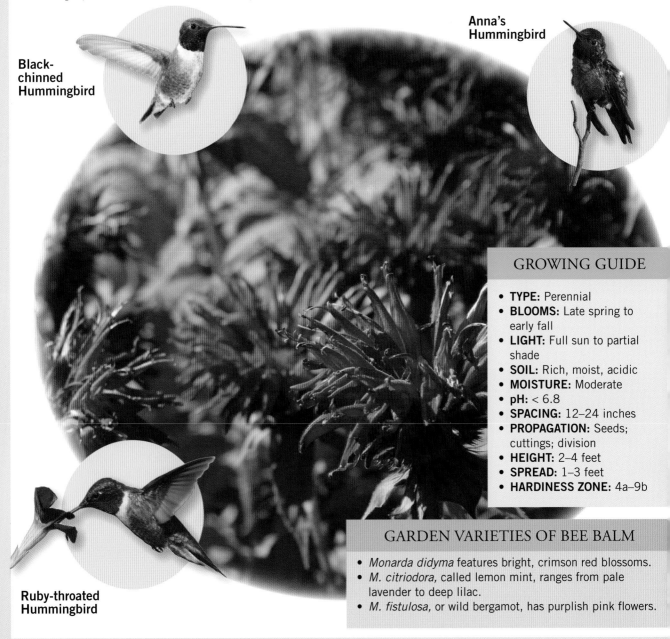

Black-chinned Hummingbird

Anna's Hummingbird

Ruby-throated Hummingbird

GROWING GUIDE

- **TYPE:** Perennial
- **BLOOMS:** Late spring to early fall
- **LIGHT:** Full sun to partial shade
- **SOIL:** Rich, moist, acidic
- **MOISTURE:** Moderate
- **pH:** < 6.8
- **SPACING:** 12–24 inches
- **PROPAGATION:** Seeds; cuttings; division
- **HEIGHT:** 2–4 feet
- **SPREAD:** 1–3 feet
- **HARDINESS ZONE:** 4a–9b

GARDEN VARIETIES OF BEE BALM

- *Monarda didyma* features bright, crimson red blossoms.
- *M. citriodora*, called lemon mint, ranges from pale lavender to deep lilac.
- *M. fistulosa*, or wild bergamot, has purplish pink flowers.

Blueberry

Genus *Vaccinium*

Birds and berries just seem to belong together, and any gardener hoping to attract feathered backyard visitors would do well to plant at least one berry-producing species. The deciduous blueberry shrub is a likely candidate because it can be cultivated anywhere in North America. It thrives in full sun, and it can reach a height of 10 feet. Its leaves are dark green, and its bell-shaped flowers are small and white. Blueberry is a popular addition to many garden landscaping plans—with so many varieties available that produce fruit at different times, you can have ripe berries in the garden from spring until fall. The sweet-smelling blueberries attract a wide range of bird species, and humans and other animals also enjoy the nutritious fruit—if there is any left after the birds have feasted!

Black-headed Grosbeak

Eastern Bluebird

Red-winged Blackbird

GROWING GUIDE

- **TYPE:** Deciduous shrub
- **BLOOMS:** Mid-spring to early summer
- **LIGHT:** Partial shade to sun
- **SOIL:** Acidic, moist
- **MOISTURE:** Above average
- **pH:** 4–5.5
- **SPACING:** 4–5 feet
- **PLANTING:** Bare root; container; balled and burlapped
- **HEIGHT:** 1–15 feet
- **SPREAD:** 8–48 inches
- **HARDINESS ZONE:** 2a–6b

GARDEN VARIETIES OF BLUEBERRY

- *Vaccinium angustifolium,* or lowbush blueberry, produces a small, sweet dark blue to black berry.
- *V. myrtilloides,* or Canadian blueberry, is one of the sweetest blueberries and produces small bright to dark blue berries.
- *V. corymbosum,* or northern highbush blueberry, produces a dark blue to black berry. *V. corymbosum* is the most common commercially produced blueberry.

California Holly

Heteromeles arbutifolia

ORDER: Rosales | FAMILY: Rosaceae

Legend has it that Hollywood was named for this evergreen bush, which once covered what are now the Hollywood Hills. California holly, also known as toyon and Christmas berry, is a decorative shrub or small tree that works well as an ornamental specimen in a bird-attracting garden. Birds will flock to the bush at the first appearance of its bright red berry clusters, which appear in the winter months and are often used as festive holiday greenery. All year round, California holly sports thick, leathery leaves; in early summer, masses of white flowers tempt butterflies, bees, and hummingbirds. Other birds use its dense cover for shelter and nesting sites.

American Robin

Hermit Thrush

Bushtit

GROWING GUIDE

- **TYPE:** Perennial
- **BLOOMS:** Late spring to early fall
- **LIGHT:** Full sun to partial shade
- **SOIL:** Rich, moist, acidic
- **MOISTURE:** Moderate
- **pH:** < 6.8
- **SPACING:** 12–24 inches
- **PROPAGATION:** Seeds; cuttings; division
- **HEIGHT:** 2–4 feet
- **SPREAD:** 1–3 feet
- **HARDINESS ZONE:** 4a–9b

Chokeberry

Genus *Aronia*

Planting ornamental shrubs that provide cover and produce long-lasting fruits is a surefire way to keep birds coming to your backyard right through the winter. The astringent-tasting, vitamin C–rich fruit of both red chokeberry and black chokeberry ripen from September to November but persist into the coldest days of January. This attractive shrub grows from 2 to 4 feet and looks great planted below larger tree species. In spring, pale pink or white flowers appear, providing nectar for insects, but this plant really shines in fall, when its leaves turn from green to bright red or purplish red. More than 20 species of birds, including chickadees, thrashers, catbirds, waxwings, and meadowlarks, enjoy chokeberries, and you will, too. Cooks can preserve them as flavorful jams and jellies.

Black-capped Chickadee

Gray Catbird

Northern Cardinal

GROWING GUIDE

- **TYPE:** Deciduous shrub
- **BLOOMS:** Spring
- **LIGHT:** Light shade to full sun
- **SOIL:** Sandy, acidic
- **MOISTURE:** Moderate
- **pH:** 5.6–7.5
- **SPACING:** 3–6 feet
- **PLANTING:** Bare root; container; balled and burlapped
- **HEIGHT:** 3–8 feet
- **SPREAD:** 3–6 feet
- **HARDINESS ZONE:** 3a–9b

Common Foxglove

Digitalis purpurea

ORDER: Lamiales | FAMILY: Plantaginacea

The densely clustered flowers of the common foxglove are pinkish purple with brown-speckled throats. Growing up to 5 feet tall, foxglove forms perfect spires of color for a cottage garden or a perennial flower bed. It is highly toxic in its natural form, but *Digitalis purpurea* is the source of the medicinal digitalis prescribed by doctors to regulate the heartbeat. This plant is a biennial, which means that it takes a year to grow and flowers the second year after planting. It is worth the wait, though. During its early summer bloom, it attracts a variety of insects and hummingbirds, which hover near the tubular blossoms drooping from a long, strong stem surrounded by a rosette of gray-green leaves. After the blooms fade, leave the plant standing. In late autumn, birds will flock to the seed heads

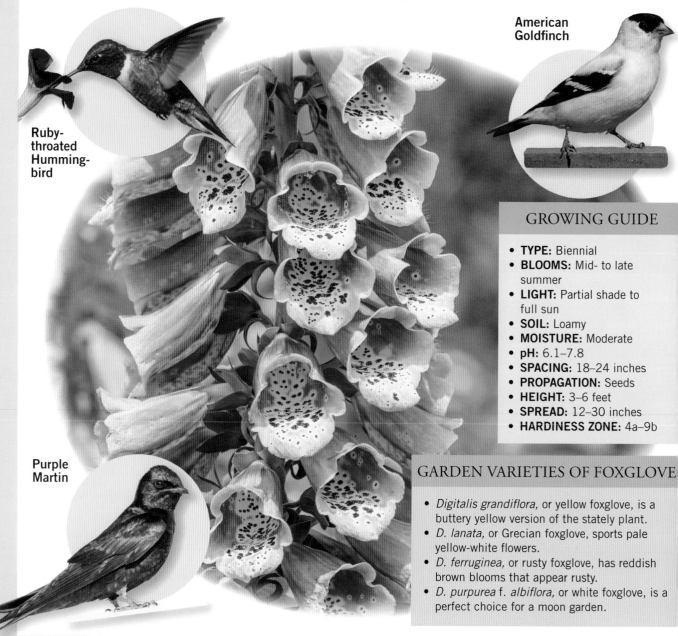

American Goldfinch

Ruby-throated Humming-bird

Purple Martin

GROWING GUIDE

- **TYPE:** Biennial
- **BLOOMS:** Mid- to late summer
- **LIGHT:** Partial shade to full sun
- **SOIL:** Loamy
- **MOISTURE:** Moderate
- **pH:** 6.1–7.8
- **SPACING:** 18–24 inches
- **PROPAGATION:** Seeds
- **HEIGHT:** 3–6 feet
- **SPREAD:** 12–30 inches
- **HARDINESS ZONE:** 4a–9b

GARDEN VARIETIES OF FOXGLOVE

- *Digitalis grandiflora,* or yellow foxglove, is a buttery yellow version of the stately plant.
- *D. lanata,* or Grecian foxglove, sports pale yellow-white flowers.
- *D. ferruginea,* or rusty foxglove, has reddish brown blooms that appear rusty.
- *D. purpurea* f. *albiflora,* or white foxglove, is a perfect choice for a moon garden.

Common Hackberry

Celtis occidentalis

ORDER: Rosales | FAMILY: Cannabaceae

Common hackberry, also known as sugarberry, nettle-tree, beaverwood, northern hackberry, and American hackberry, is a triple-threat bird lure: it offers food, shelter, and a place to nest to more than 50 species. Hackberry is a deciduous tree that can withstand long periods without water. It produces small fuzzy green flowers in early spring, and its small, singular berries ripen in summer and often persist into winter. A wide range of birds, including thrashers, robins, woodpeckers, and wood warblers, thrive on hackberries, which range in color from orange-red to dark purple. Butterflies also frequent these trees, providing an additional source of food for backyard birds.

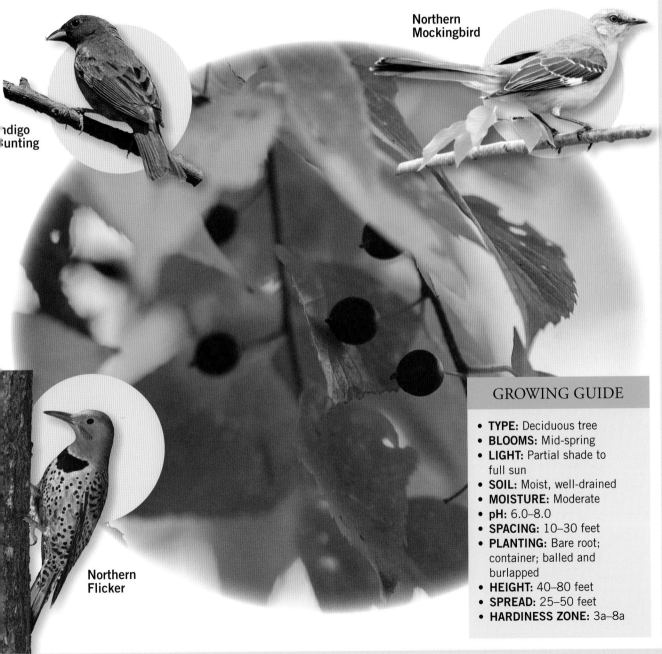

Indigo Bunting

Northern Mockingbird

Northern Flicker

GROWING GUIDE

- **TYPE:** Deciduous tree
- **BLOOMS:** Mid-spring
- **LIGHT:** Partial shade to full sun
- **SOIL:** Moist, well-drained
- **MOISTURE:** Moderate
- **pH:** 6.0–8.0
- **SPACING:** 10–30 feet
- **PLANTING:** Bare root; container; balled and burlapped
- **HEIGHT:** 40–80 feet
- **SPREAD:** 25–50 feet
- **HARDINESS ZONE:** 3a–8a

Cosmos

Cosmos bipinnatus

Cosmos is a colorful herbaceous plant that gets one of its nicknames, Mexican aster, from its native land. These days, however, it is a garden staple over much of North America, chosen for its vivid purple, white, pink, or red blooms and delicate, threadlike leaves of bright green. Cosmos, also called garden cosmos, is an easy plant to grow: all this disease-resistant plant needs is some sunlight and it only requires watering in drought conditions. Its flowers attract a multitude of butterflies, and as the bloom die off, they reveal abundant seeds for birds to enjoy. Although cosmos is an annual, the plant self-sows its seeds and will return year after year.

Dark-eyed Junco

House Finch

Song Sparrow

GROWING GUIDE

- **TYPE:** Annual
- **BLOOMS:** Late spring to fall
- **LIGHT:** Full sun
- **SOIL:** Well-drained
- **MOISTURE:** Moderate
- **pH:** 6.6–8.5
- **SPACING:** 12–24 inches
- **PROPAGATION:** Seeds
- **HEIGHT:** 2–4 feet
- **SPREAD:** 1–3 feet
- **HARDINESS ZONE:** 5a–10b

Crabapple

Genus *Malus*

The dusky red or golden yellow pome of the crabapple tree tends to be sour, and humans rarely consume it in its raw state. Birds, on the other hand, happily feed on this woody fruit. The crabapple is a great choice for a bird-friendly backyard: nearly 30 avian species, including songbirds, robins, waxwings, and woodpeckers, visit its branches in the fall in search of a meal. In spring, as the crabapple begins its display of red, pink, or white flowers, hummingbirds hover at the blooms to sip their nectar, and other birds visit the branches in search of nesting sites. The crabapple's combination of edible fruit and eye-catching flowers help to make it a popular ornamental tree or shrub.

Red-headed Woodpecker

Gray Catbird

Cedar Waxwing

GROWING GUIDE

- **TYPE:** Deciduous tree
- **BLOOMS:** Early to late spring
- **LIGHT:** Partial shade to full sun
- **SOIL:** Moist, well-drained
- **MOISTURE:** Moderate
- **pH:** 5.0–6.5
- **SPACING:** 20–40 feet
- **PLANTING:** Bare root; container; balled and burlapped
- **HEIGHT:** 8–40 feet
- **SPREAD:** 15–20 feet
- **HARDINESS ZONE:** 4b–9a

GARDEN VARIETIES OF CRABAPPLE

- *Malus angustifolia,* or southern crabapple, is extremely acidic but cooks up into delicious jellies, jams, and preserves.
- *M. coronaria,* or sweet crabapple, produces fragrant rose-colored blossoms.
- *M. fusca,* known as Oregon crabapple or Pacific crabapple, is eaten raw or cooked.

Dogwood

Genus *Cornus*

Dogwood derives its name from the word *dagwood*, which is a reference to its strong, daggerlike wood. There are many flowering species of dogwood, but in North America, *Cornus florida* dominates, and home-owners often plant it as an ornamental shrub or a tree. Dogwood's attractive, closely clustered flowers are white, yellow, or pink. Its fruit, called drupes, are primarily red, but they can appear in blue or white, too. Fleshy dogwood drupes form a nutritious food supply for many species of birds, including bluebirds, cardinals, buntings, kingbirds, thrushes, vireos, and wood warblers. Many birds also hunt for insects in the bark. Dogwood blooms attracts many types of butterflies and moths, which greatly enhance its value as a bird-attracting specimen in your garden.

House Wren

Western Kingbird

Pileated Woodpecker

GROWING GUIDE

- **TYPE:** Deciduous tree
- **BLOOMS:** Mid-spring
- **LIGHT:** Partial shade to full sun
- **SOIL:** Moist
- **MOISTURE:** Moderate
- **pH:** 5.6–6.5
- **SPACING:** 15–20 feet
- **PLANTING:** Bare root; container; balled and burlapped
- **HEIGHT:** 15–30 feet
- **SPREAD:** 20–35 feet
- **HARDINESS ZONE:** 5a–9a

GARDEN VARIETIES OF DOGWOOD

- *Cornus florida,* or flowering dogwood, has a multitude of cultivars, with flowers ranging in color from snowy white to strong pink, and bears bright red berries.
- *C. amomum,* or silky dogwood, produces white drupes.
- *C. sericea,* or red-osier dogwood, bears clusters of white berries in the fall.

Eastern Redcedar

uniperus virginiana

Juniperus virginiana goes by many names—red cedar, eastern juniper, red juniper, pencil cedar, and, most often, eastern redcedar. More than 50 bird species, including juncos, robins, sparrows, swallows, wood warblers, and axwings, visit this tree to eat its fruit, shelter in its foliage, nd build nests in its branches. The Cedar Waxwing even ets its name from this tree, which is not really a cedar, but instead a fairly small, shrubby juniper. With green needles and reddish bark, it makes a colorful statement in a snow-covered backyard. Its seed cones look like small berries and are dark, purplish blue with a waxy white coating that turns them powder blue. These "berries" feed many birds during the cold months. In warmer climates, the eastern redcedar provides dense shelter for wintering hummingbirds.

ee wallow

Cedar Waxwing

Yellow Warbler

GROWING GUIDE

- **TYPE:** Evergreen conifer
- **BLOOMS:** Late spring
- **LIGHT:** Full sun
- **SOIL:** Moist
- **MOISTURE:** Moderate
- **pH:** 6.0–8.0
- **SPACING:** 3–6 feet
- **PLANTING:** Bare root; container; balled and burlapped
- **HEIGHT:** 20–60 feet
- **SPREAD:** 15–30 feet
- **HARDINESS ZONE:** 2a–9b

29

Elder

Genus Sambucus

ORDER: Dipsacales | FAMILY: Adoxacea

Also known as elderberry or black elder, elder is grown as a wide variety of shrubs and small trees. Its leaves are feather-shaped, and in springtime, it bears large clusters of creamy white flowers. The flowers add flavor to cordials, and the berries are used to make wine, jelly, and jam. The small dark blue, purple, or black berries appear in the summer months, growing in drooping clumps and attracting a wide range of fruit-eating birds. Elderberries are a source of nutrients not only for birds but also for many types of insects, which the birds may also eat. Elder offers nesting sites, too, making it one of the most bird-friendly trees or shrubs for any yard, attracting catbirds, thrashers, kinglets, finches, towhees, woodpeckers, cardinals, orioles, robins, grosbeaks, and waxwings.

Golden-crowned Kinglet

Red-eyed Vireo

Tufted Titmouse

GROWING GUIDE

- **TYPE:** Deciduous shrub
- **BLOOMS:** Midsummer
- **LIGHT:** Partial shade to full sun
- **SOIL:** Adaptable
- **MOISTURE:** Moderate
- **pH:** 5.2–7.2
- **SPACING:** 8–10 feet
- **PLANTING:** Bare root; container; balled and burlapped
- **HEIGHT:** 10–30 feet
- **SPREAD:** 8–20 feet
- **HARDINESS ZONE:** 3a–9b

European Black Alder

Alnus glutinosa

ORDER: Fagales | FAMILY: Betulaceae

Despite its name, European black alder is a common North American shade tree, chosen for its fast growth and ornamental appeal. Its leathery oval leaves stay green late into the fall, when woody cone-shaped catkins join them. In October and November, the greenish catkins open and turn brown. The catkins contain small nutlets, which persist through the winter and provide many birds with a reliable cold-weather food supply. Finches, jays, tanagers, grosbeaks, sapsuckers, wood warblers, and many other species enjoy the seeds of the European black alder. Some of them also feast on the sap within the trunk or the insects on its foliage. Many species of birds also use its branches for their nesting sites, making this alder a strong choice for a bird-watcher's backyard.

White-breasted Nuthatch

Summer Tanager

Pine Siskin

GROWING GUIDE

- **TYPE:** Deciduous tree
- **BLOOMS:** Early spring
- **LIGHT:** Partial shade to full sun
- **SOIL:** Moist to wet
- **MOISTURE:** Above average
- **pH:** 5.1–7.8
- **SPACING:** 30–40 feet
- **PLANTING:** Bare root; container; balled and burlapped
- **HEIGHT:** 40–60 feet
- **SPREAD:** 20–40 feet
- **HARDINESS ZONE:** 3a–7b

Hosta

Genus *Hosta*

ORDER: Asparagales | FAMILY: Agavacea[

With a score or two of species, the genus *Hosta* comprises a long list of shade-garden beauties. Useful as a lush ground cover, hosta also attracts a variety of birds, including flycatchers, orioles, and swallows. Although lovely white to violet flowers appear, usually in late summer, its leaves are its main attraction. Broad oval to long and lance-shaped, the leaves seem to burst from abundant spiraling clumps. Leaf colors range from yellow-green to true green to deep blue-green. Variegated specimens, in combinations like kelly green leaves with cream piping or gold leaves with white edges and centers, add to this long-lived and easy-care plant's appeal.

Barn Swallow

Great Crested Flycatcher

Baltimore Oriole

GROWING GUIDE

- **TYPE:** Perennial
- **BLOOMS:** Summer
- **LIGHT:** Light to full shade
- **SOIL:** Moist, well-drained
- **MOISTURE:** Moderate
- **pH:** 6.5–7.5
- **SPACING:** 1–3 feet
- **PROPAGATION:** Division; seeds
- **HEIGHT:** 6–36 inches
- **SPREAD:** 12–36 inches
- **HARDINESS ZONE:** 3a–8b

HOSTA CULTIVARS

- 'Buckshaw Blue' is medium-size, with heart-shaped blue leaves and very pale blue flowers.
- 'Francee' is large, with dark green leaves edged in white and lavender flowers.
- 'Golden Sunburst' is large, with chartreuse leaves and white flowers.
- 'Honeybells' is large, with light green leaves and fragrant white-mauve flowers.
- 'Sagae' is large, with frosted green leaves edged in cream and pale yellow flowers.

Lilac

Syringa vulgaris

Lilac is a deciduous flowering shrub belonging to the olive family. In addition to the color by the same name, lilac flowers can appear in tones of pink, white, magenta, and yellow. This shrub is a garden classic, loved for its beauty and its heady fragrance. Heavy clusters of four-petaled flowers begin to bloom in spring and continue into the summer months. The bark of the lilac shrub is smooth and gray. The warmer months are the best time of year to enjoy this plant, which loses much of its allure by the time autumn arrives. Lilacs are especially attractive to hummingbirds and butterflies. Its seeds attract cardinals, chickadees, and finches.

Blue Grosbeak

Black-chinned Hummingbird

Black-capped Chickadee

GROWING GUIDE

- **TYPE:** Deciduous shrub
- **BLOOMS:** Late spring, early summer
- **LIGHT:** Full sun
- **SOIL:** Well-drained, slightly acidic
- **MOISTURE:** Moderate
- **pH:** 6.1–7.5
- **SPACING:** 10–12 feet
- **PLANTING:** Bare root; container; balled and burlapped
- **HEIGHT:** 8–15 feet
- **SPREAD:** 6–12 feet
- **HARDINESS ZONE:** 3a–7b

LILAC CULTIVARS

- 'Lavender Lady' blooms with panicles of fragrant lavender florets.
- 'Charles Joly' is a classic version with deep magenta flowers.
- 'Edith Cavell' has clusters of showy, double, white flowers.
- 'President Lincoln' sports loose clusters of nearly true-blue flowers.

Norway Spruce

Picea abies

ORDER: Pinales | FAMILY: Pinace

This European native owes some of its North American popularity to its reputation as a magnificent Christmas tree. A Norway spruce, which can reach 100 feet in height, is the typical choice to grace New York City's Rockefeller Center during the holiday season. You may be lucky enough to have an established Norway spruce on your property, but if not, it's easy to plant one. A fast-growing and disease-resistant conifer, it has a charming cone-shaped silhouette and spiky green needles. When the tree matures, the red-brown cones, so loved by birds, will begin to develop in the canopy. More than 25 bird species including nuthatches, finches, crossbills, and chickadees, look to this tree for food, shelter, and nesting sites, and w appreciate finding a Norway spruce in your backyard.

Red-breasted Nuthatch

Steller's Jay

Red Crossbill

GROWING GUIDE

- **TYPE:** Evergreen conifer
- **BLOOMS:** Mid-spring to midsummer
- **LIGHT:** Full sun
- **SOIL:** Moist, sandy, well-drained
- **MOISTURE:** Moderate
- **pH:** 5.6–7.5
- **SPACING:** 20–30 feet
- **PLANTING:** Bare root; container; balled and burlapped
- **HEIGHT:** 40–100 feet
- **SPREAD:** 25–40 feet
- **HARDINESS ZONE:** 3b–8b

Purple Coneflower

Echinacea purpurea

ORDER: Asterales | FAMILY: Asteraceae

Find a sunny spot in your garden for this hardy, daisy-like perennial, and watch hummingbirds, bees, and butterflies flock to its showy flowers. And showy they are, with raised brown cones surrounded by drooping tutus of pinkish mauve petals. Purple coneflower is an easy-to-grow prairie native that is pest- and disease-resistant. With its long blooming season, you will have plenty of cut flowers to enjoy in summer bouquets, with enough plants left over to attract songbirds and finches to your garden after the flowers go to seed. Because of its large head, it produces a multitude of seeds that will keep birds nourished well into the fall. In late fall or early winter, trim purple coneflower down to the ground; by the next spring, the birds will have a new food source.

American Goldfinch

Black-chinned Hummingbird

Eastern Bluebird

GROWING GUIDE

- **TYPE:** Perennial
- **BLOOMS:** Midsummer to fall
- **LIGHT:** Partial shade to full sun
- **SOIL:** Well-drained
- **MOISTURE:** Moderate
- **pH:** 6.1–7.8
- **SPACING:** 24–48 inches
- **PROPAGATION:** Seeds
- **HEIGHT:** 2–6 feet
- **SPREAD:** 1–2 feet
- **HARDINESS ZONE:** 2a–10b

PURPLE CONEFLOWER CULTIVARS

- 'Coconut Lime' is a pale lime green with an orange cone.
- 'Doubledecker' wears a two-tiered skirt: a shorter skirt flares out from the top of the brown cone and a longer one, with deep rose-pink petals, flutters from the base.
- 'Fatal Attraction' features a nearly black stem and a deep brown cone surrounded by magenta petals.

Serviceberry

Genus *Amelanchier*

ORDER: Rosales | FAMILY: Rosacea

This deciduous woodland tree is a popular garden landscaping choice, with its breathtaking fall display of luminous yellow and red leaves. It begins its fruitful season in spring, however, with delicate white flowers, which are telltale reminders that warmer weather is approaching. The short-lived blossoms remain on the bush for only a week or two before they fall away. Then the purple fruit of the tree begins to grow, ripening in about three weeks. Serviceberr takes two to three years to fully mature and produce fruit, which attracts scores of birds, including phoebes, flickers, chickadees, mockingbirds, cardinals, towhees, thrushes, woodpeckers, waxwings, bluebirds, vireos, grosbeaks, thrashers, and titmice. Humans can eat this fragrant fruit, too, which tastes similar to blueberry.

Rose-breasted Grosbeak

Eastern Phoebe

Downy Woodpecker

GROWING GUIDE

- **TYPE:** Deciduous large shrub/small tree
- **BLOOMS:** Early to mid-spring
- **LIGHT:** Partial shade to full sun
- **SOIL:** Moist, well-drained
- **MOISTURE:** Above average
- **pH:** 5.6–7.8
- **SPACING:** 4–6 feet
- **PLANTING:** Bare root; container; balled and burlapped
- **HEIGHT:** 6–20 feet
- **SPREAD:** 10–20 feet
- **HARDINESS ZONE:** 3a–8b

Sugar Maple

cer saccharum

ORDER: Sapindales | FAMILY: Sapindaceae

he sugar maple is a New England trademark, with its impressive spread, striking fall color, and sap, which pplies the world with maple syrup and sugar. Besides tisfying the human sweet tooth, the sugar maple offers uch to birds. Some, such as cardinals, bobwhites, and osbeaks, use this tree as a food source. Others, such as orioles, nest in its branches. Still others, including vireos, robins, and goldfinches, use it as a combination of hiding place and nesting site. A valuable addition to a birder's landscape, the sugar maple needs space, sun, and well-drained soil—if you can offer these, you will supply many birds with all of life's necessities: food, shelter, and nesting.

Black-and-white Warbler

Brown Creeper

White-breasted Nuthatch

GROWING GUIDE

- **TYPE:** Deciduous tree
- **BLOOMS:** Mid-spring
- **LIGHT:** Partial to full sun
- **SOIL:** Loamy, well-drained, moist
- **MOISTURE:** Moderate
- **pH:** 3.7–7.3
- **SPACING:** 50–60 trees per acre
- **PLANTING:** Bare root; container; balled and burlapped
- **HEIGHT:** 70–90 feet
- **SPREAD:** 60–80 feet
- **HARDINESS ZONE:** 3a–8

Sunflower

Helianthus annuus

ORDER: Asterales | FAMILY: Asteraceae

The common sunflower is an annual found in many North American gardens. Its large, cheerful yellow flower heads produce an abundance of fruit, known as sunflower seeds. Birds thrive on them; in fact, sunflower seeds are one of the most plentiful food sources for birds all over the world, feeding finches, nuthatches, chickadees, sparrows, cardinals, titmice, and juncos. Its low-maintenance upkeep also contributes to the sunflower's popularity. Even a novice gardener can grow this spectacular plant with minimal effort and care. Sunflowers can grow very tall, and some varieties reach more than 8 feet in height, with flower heads of nearly a foot in diameter.

Indigo Bunting

Song Sparrow

Mourning Dove

GROWING GUIDE

- **TYPE:** Annual
- **BLOOMS:** Midsummer to fall
- **LIGHT:** Full sun
- **SOIL:** Moist, well-drained
- **MOISTURE:** Moderate
- **pH:** 5.7–8.0
- **SPACING:** 9–12 inches
- **PROPAGATION:** Seeds
- **HEIGHT:** 2–10 feet
- **SPREAD:** 3–6 inches
- **HARDINESS ZONE:** 3a–11

Switchgrass

anicum virgatum

witchgrass is a common, easy-to-maintain ornamental grass that is native to North America. It also goes by the names "panic grass" and "prairie tall grass," the latter because it is abundant in the prairies of the Midwest United States. Its adaptability to partial shade, poor soil conditions, and erratic weather makes this plant an easy-re addition to a garden. Switchgrass is straight and sturdy, providing grassland birds, such as meadowlarks, quails, bobolinks, and sparrows, with food, cover, and nesting materials. It produces many tiny seeds, which makes it a wonderful foraging plant for birds. In the autumn months, switchgrass changes from bluish green to reddish purple and produces small purple blooms. Ornamental switchgrass reaches between 3 and 7 feet when it is in flower.

Lark Sparrow

Western Meadowlark

Bobolink

GROWING GUIDE

- **TYPE:** Perennial grass
- **BLOOMS:** Late spring to early summer
- **LIGHT:** Partial shade to full sun
- **SOIL:** Loamy, sandy
- **MOISTURE:** Moderate to dry
- **pH:** 6.1–7.8
- **SPACING:** N/A
- **PROPAGATION:** Division; seeds
- **HEIGHT:** 3–5 feet
- **SPREAD:** N/A
- **HARDINESS ZONE:** 5a–9b

Trumpet Honeysuckle

Lonicera sempervirens

ORDER: Dipsacales | FAMILY: Caprifoliacea

Hummingbirds can't resist this semievergreen vine's eye-catching flowers. The trumpet-shaped blooms are 2 inches long and tinged deep coral, hence its other common name: coral honeysuckle. Trumpet honeysuckle makes a bold statement twining up a trellis or winding over an arbor. In warm climates, the flowers appear in spring and persist all summer long, but even in colder areas, such as the Northeast, trumpet honeysuckle may bloom sporadically until fall, if the weather stays warm. Hummingbirds and orioles will drop by to sip on the flowers' nectar. In fall, some of the flowers produce bright red fruits that will lure songbirds to your garden.

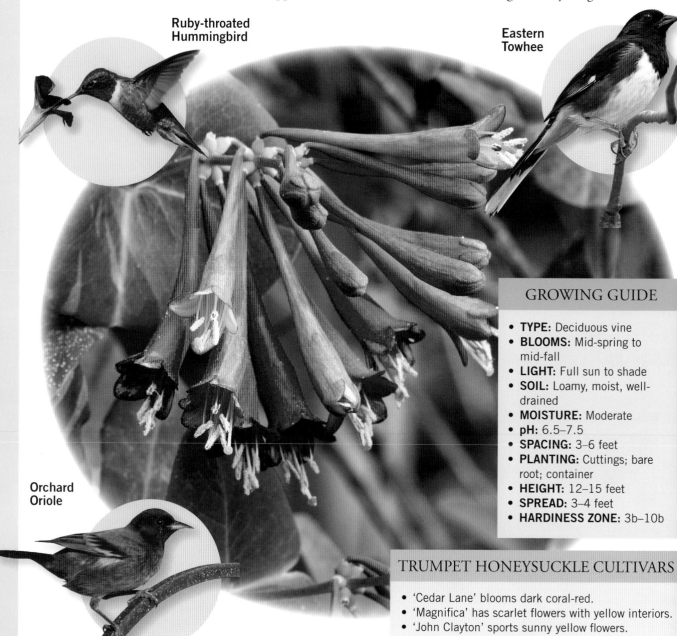

Ruby-throated Hummingbird

Eastern Towhee

Orchard Oriole

GROWING GUIDE

- **TYPE:** Deciduous vine
- **BLOOMS:** Mid-spring to mid-fall
- **LIGHT:** Full sun to shade
- **SOIL:** Loamy, moist, well-drained
- **MOISTURE:** Moderate
- **pH:** 6.5–7.5
- **SPACING:** 3–6 feet
- **PLANTING:** Cuttings; bare root; container
- **HEIGHT:** 12–15 feet
- **SPREAD:** 3–4 feet
- **HARDINESS ZONE:** 3b–10b

TRUMPET HONEYSUCKLE CULTIVARS

- 'Cedar Lane' blooms dark coral-red.
- 'Magnifica' has scarlet flowers with yellow interiors.
- 'John Clayton' sports sunny yellow flowers.

Zinnia

Genus *Zinnia*

Zinnia's neon hues attract gardeners and birds alike. With more than 20 species and scores of cultivars, which range in size from dwarf 8-inch specimens to impressive 48-inch plants, this annual is a deserving addition to summer flower beds, window boxes, and other outdoor planters. It is an easy-care plant, and it does especially well during long, hot summers. It greatest value to the bird-watching gardener, however, is its ability to lure birds to your yard. Hummingbirds will stop by to sip its nectar, and so, too, will butterflies. After its flowering season, do not deadhead the blooms—zinnias produce great big seeds that many birds love, including finches and other songbirds.

White-crowned Sparrow

House Finch

Dark-eyed Junco

GROWING GUIDE

- **TYPE:** Annual
- **BLOOMS:** Late summer to early fall
- **LIGHT:** Full sun
- **SOIL:** Well-drained
- **MOISTURE:** Moderate
- **pH:** 6.1–7.8
- **SPACING:** 9–12 inches
- **PROPAGATION:** Seeds
- **HEIGHT:** 8–48 inches
- **SPREAD:** 10–24 inches
- **HARDINESS ZONE:** 3–10

ZINNIA CULTIVARS

- 'Persian Carpet' grows to 15 inches, with double, bicolored flower heads of gold, maroon, purple, chocolate, pink, or cream.
- 'Old Mexico' reaches 18 inches, with double blooms in rich mahogany highlighted with yellow-gold.
- 'Peter Pan' is a dwarf zinnia available in pink, scarlet, gold, cream, and flame.

Steller's Jay

Cedar Waxwings

House Wren

Downy Woodpecker

en-crowned Kinglet

A Gardener's Guide to Favorite Backyard Birds

-throated Hummingbird

Crossbills

Tufted Titmouse

House Wren

Troglodytes aedon

ORDER: Passeriformes | FAMILY: Troglodytidæ

This small, shy bird's cheerful song can be heard in backyards throughout North America, particularly during its mating season. Its song differs regionally from the north to the west, where a unique tone and rhythm define each variation. The adult House Wren's unassuming plumage is brown on its back with blackish barring on its wings and tail; its underside is a lighter, grayish brown.

The House Wren's beak is long and narrow, and its tail is short and often cocked. A hole burrowed into a tree by a woodpecker is one of its favorite nesting sites. This feisty bird also enjoys the comfort of a birdhouse so much that it is known to usurp the human-made houses of other birds. The enterprising and opportunistic House Wren also nests in such places as mailboxes and flowerpots.

House Wren (adult)

House Wren feeding chick

FOWL FACTS & FIGURES

LENGTH RANGE: 4–5 inches

WEIGHT: 0.4 ounce

WINGSPAN: 6–7 inches

SONG OR CALL: Song is a long, bubbly cascade of doubled notes and trills. Call is a variety of *churrs*, rattles, chatters, and a scolding *cheh-cheh*.

NEST: Cup-shaped nest of twigs, sticks, and grass lined with feathers, wool, and other soft material, filling a cavity such as a nest box

EGGS:
Color: White with brown flecks
Incubation: 13–15 days
Clutch Size: 5–8 eggs

WHERE ARE THEY?

LEGEND
- Year Round
- Summer (breeding)
- Winter (nonbreeding)
- Migration

BEST TREES AND PLANTS FOR YOUR GARDEN

❶ Sugar maple (*Acer saccharum*) ❷ Blackjack oak (*Quercus marilandica*) ❸ Coralberry (*Ardisia crispa*) ❹ American hazelnut (*Corylus americana*) ❺ Greenleaf manzanita (*Arctostaphylos patula*): A sugar maple tree will provide an ideal foraging spot for the House Wren, while blackjack oak, with its leathery triangular leaves, will give it a place to nest. The blackjack oak is particularly lovely in spring when its young bell-shaped leaves are tinged pinkish red. Dense deciduous shrubs, such as coralberry and American hazelnut, are favorite foraging places for this bird. For drier climates, a greenleaf manzanita shrub is a good choice for your garden. Its thick foliage, stunning flowers, and berries have high visual appeal, and it also attracts insects for the House Wren to eat.

HOW TO ATTRACT HOUSE WRENS

- Plant plenty of ground-cover vegetation.
- Mount a wren house or a hollow gourd for roosting and nesting; alternatively, do not clear away dead wood that contains old woodpecker holes.
- Erect a small, shallow birdbath in your garden.

FAVORITE FOODS

Insects

Spiders

Lark Sparrow

Chondestes grammacus

ORDER: Passeriformes | FAMILY: Emberizida

The Lark Sparrow is the sole member of the genus *Chondestes*. It is a large sparrow, native to southern Canada and most of the United States. The male and female look alike, with chestnut cheeks and a striped crown of black, chestnut, and white. A characteristic dark spot at the center of its chest helps distinguish the Lark Sparrow from other sparrows. It thrives in a grassland habitat with scrubby shrubs or in areas with poor or sandy soil, where i feeds on a diet of insects and seeds. The male Lark Sparrow is one of the few songbirds that walk instead of hop, and it will only hop when trying to attract a mate. The song of this sparrow is a melodic sequence of buzzes and trills.

Lark Sparrow (adult)

Lark Sparrow, showing chest spot

FOWL FACTS & FIGURES

LENGTH RANGE: 6–7 inches

WEIGHT: 1 ounce

WINGSPAN: 11 inches

SONG OR CALL: Song is a melodic series of trills, buzzes, pauses, and clear notes. Call is a sharp *tik*.

NEST: Sticks and grass located in bushes, shrubs, thickets, and grasslands

EGGS:
Color: White or pale gray with brown and black flecks
Incubation: 11–12 days
Clutch Size: 3–6 eggs

WHERE ARE THEY?

LEGEND
- Year Round
- Summer (breeding)
- Winter (nonbreeding)
- Migration

BEST TREES AND PLANTS FOR YOUR GARDEN

❶ **Brittlebush (*Encelia farinosa*)** ❷ **Black-eyed Susan (*Rudbeckia hirta*)** ❸ **Coralbells (genus *Heuchera*)** ❹ **Little bluestem (*Schizachyrium scoparium*):** Brittlebush is an ornamental desert shrub with brilliant yellow flowers that burst into bloom in early spring. It produces a rich supply of seeds and attracts a variety of insects for the Lark Sparrow to eat. Black-eyed Susan is a cottage-garden classic, with deep yellow-gold petals surrounding the dark brown, seed-rich flower head that birds will pick clean. Coralbells, which blossom in clusters of bell-shaped flowers in varying shades of pink, provide good ground cover for foraging. Little bluestem is a native grass that grows well even in poor soil. It provides both protective cover and nourishing seeds.

HOW TO ATTRACT LARK SPARROWS

Creeping phlox

- Set up a birdbath. The Lark Sparrow likes to bathe and will drink from a birdbath, too.
- Plant herbaceous ground covers, such as creeping phlox *(Phlox subulata)* and foamflowers *(Tiarella cordifolia)*; these two species grow very well together.
- Plant a hedgerow along the perimeter of your yard to create an ideal habitat for this bird.

FAVORITE FOODS

Seeds

Insects

Song Sparrow

Melospiza melodia

ORDER: Passeriformes | FAMILY: Emberizida

This common brown North American garden bird has a gray face with distinctive striping and a conical bill. Its tail is long and rounded. The Song Sparrow is attracted to marshy or brushy areas and thrives on a diet of insects, seeds, and, occasionally, small crustaceans. It gathers food by foraging in shrubs or in shallow bodies of water. This sparrow is the improv artist of the bird world, singing as many as 1,000 variations on its basic 20-song repertoire. The male voices these complex songs to protect and defen its territory. It learns its songs from other Song Sparrows i the immediate area, which makes it nearly impossible for other birds to mimic them. Similarly, the Song Sparrow's appearance also varies greatly according to its geographica location, and there are dozens of subspecies.

Song Sparrow (adult)

Juvenile Song Sparrow

FOWL FACTS & FIGURES

LENGTH RANGE: 5–7 inches

WEIGHT: 1 ounce

WINGSPAN: 7–10 inches

SONG OR CALL: Song is a varied trill, sounding similar to *Madge-Madge-Madge, put-on-your-tea-kettle-ettle-ettle.*

NEST: Cup-shaped nest made of grass, forbs, leaves, and bark strips, lined with finer materials, sited beneath grass tufts, shrubs, or brush piles

EGGS:
Color: Pale blue to greenish white with reddish brown marks
Incubation: 12–14 days
Clutch Size: 2–6 eggs

WHERE ARE THEY?

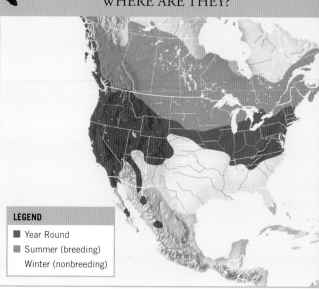

LEGEND
■ Year Round
■ Summer (breeding)
  Winter (nonbreeding)

BEST TREES AND PLANTS FOR YOUR GARDEN

❶ Withe-rod (*Viburnum nudum* var. *cassinoides*)
❷ Euonymus (genus *Euonymus*) ❸ Creeping cotoneaster
(*Cotoneaster adpressus*) ❹ Red hot poker (*Kniphofia uvaria*):
The withe-rod shrub provides the Song Sparrow with an appealing
place to nest, and it adds color to the garden all year round. In
summer, its creamy flowers bloom; in fall, its leaves burst into shades
of red and purple. Withe-rod's berries, which change from green
to rose-pink to blue to purplish black, last into the winter months.
Euonymus berries contain seeds that the Song Sparrow eats, and
its blossoms lure insects into the garden. You can grow euonymus,
sometimes called "spindles," as a shrub or a small tree. Creeping
cotoneaster is a low-growing shrub with glossy green leaves that
provide cover and foraging territory for the Song Sparrow. In late
summer, creeping cotoneaster bursts into color with brilliant crimson
berries. To add a burst of fiery color and supply the Song Sparrow
with seeds, add a grouping of red hot poker to your garden. This
torch-shaped flower shades from lemon yellow to flaming scarlet. It
grows to 5 feet in height.

HOW TO ATTRACT SONG SPARROWS

- Scatter seeds on the ground.
- Install a birdbath, a pond, or a fountain in your yard.
- Plant dense shrubs to provide habitat for foraging and cover.

FAVORITE FOODS

Berries　　Grains　　Seeds　　Insects

White-crowned Sparrow

Zonotrichia leucophrys

ORDER: Passeriformes | FAMILY: Emberizida

The White-crowned Sparrow, recognized by its tan back feathers, tan wings with white wing bars, gray underbelly, and very long tail, winters in much of North America. Its face is gray; its eyes are dark; and it has distinctive stripes of black and white on its head. Using a two-footed scratching technique, this sparrow forages on the ground for seeds and insects, such as caterpillars and beetles, but sometimes catches flying insects, such as wasp from a tree perch. It is a social bird, traveling and foraging in flocks, especially in winter. Its song is a mix of buzzes and trills introduced by a sweet melodic whistle. The song of each White-crowned Sparrow is specific to its subspecie and its geographic region, and it learns its distinct native song, or "dialect," within the first few months of its life.

White-crowned Sparrow (adult)

Juvenile White-crowned Sparrow

FOWL FACTS & FIGURES

LENGTH RANGE: 6–7 inches

WEIGHT: 1 ounce

WINGSPAN: 8–9.5 inches

SONG OR CALL: Song is a melodic series of trills, buzzes, and whistles. Call is a variety of sounds, including *poor-wet-wetter-chee-zee* and *tseek.*

NEST: Cup-shaped nest made of sticks and grass lined with finer grass or animal hair located in bushes, shrubs, thickets, and grasslands

EGGS:
Color: Light blue or green with red-brown marks
Incubation: 11–14 days
Clutch Size: 2–6 eggs

WHERE ARE THEY?

LEGEND

■ Year Round
■ Summer (breeding)
□ Winter (nonbreeding)
▨ Migration

BEST TREES AND PLANTS FOR YOUR GARDEN

❶ Burning bush (*Euonymus alatus*) ❷ Blackberry (genus *Rubus*) ❸ Common elder (*Sambucus nigra*): As do many sparrows, the White-crowned Sparrow eats the berries of the decorative burning bush, known for its fiery fall color. This tough plant can thrive in both urban and suburban areas, making it a popular landscaping choice. It would not be unusual to catch sight of a White-crowned Sparrow or two wintering within the thorny bramble branches in your yard. It will also eat the blackberries that appear on brambles in late summer. Blackberries are really dense clusters of drupes that shade from green to red to purple-black as they ripen. In summer, common elder produces dark, juicy berries that the White-crowned Sparrow will devour.

HOW TO ATTRACT WHITE-CROWNED SPARROWS

- Position a tray bird feeder low to the ground, and fill it with black-oil sunflower seeds and red and white millet. White-crowned Sparrows will also eat peanuts and bread crumbs.
- Encourage plants in your yard that produce grains, and introduce grasses and berry bushes.
- Plant a cluster of shrubs for nesting and foraging.

FAVORITE FOODS

Berries   **Grains**   **Insects**

Dark-eyed Junco

Junco hyemalis

ORDER: Passeriformes | FAMILY: Emberizida

The Dark-eyed Junco is a species of North American sparrow that summers in Alaska and the northern territories of Canada. It is commonly referred to as a "snowbird." It spends its winters farther south, where you will often observe it in suburban gardens. Its coloration varies, but it usually has a black "hood," dark eyes, pink bill, gray or brown back, white underbelly, and distinctive white-rimmed tail. The male and the female look similar, although the male may have more conspicuous markings. Its diet consists mainly of seeds and insects, which it gathers by hopping along on the ground. The Dark-eyed Junco has several subspecies, all of which were once considered separate species: Slate-colored Junco (photo opposite bottom), Oregon Junco, Pink-sided Junco, Gray-headed Junco, and White-winged Junco. These subspecies often intermingle when flying or foraging for food.

Male Dark-eyed Junco (adult Oregon Junco)

Female Dark-eyed Junco (Slate-colored Junco)

FOWL FACTS & FIGURES

LENGTH RANGE: 5.5–6.3 inches

WEIGHT: 0.7–1 ounce

WINGSPAN: 7–10 inches

SONG OR CALL: Song is metallic trill. Call is a variety of sounds, including *dit, tsick,* and *tchet.*

NEST: A well-hidden cup-shaped depression on the ground lined with fine grasses and hair or, more rarely, in the lower branches of a shrub or tree

EGGS:
Color: Grayish white or very pale blue with splotches of brown
Incubation: 11–13 days
Clutch Size: 3–6 eggs

WHERE ARE THEY?

LEGEND
- Year Round
- Summer (breeding)
- Winter (nonbreeding)

BEST TREES AND PLANTS FOR YOUR GARDEN

❶ Chrysanthemum (genus *Chrysanthemum*) ❷ Zinnia (genus *Zinnia*) ❸ Marigold (genus *Tagetes*) ❹ American sweetgum (*Liquidambar styracifluar*): Flowers are among your best choices of plants if you want to attract ground foragers like the Dark-eyed Junco to your garden. The perennial chrysanthemum will attract many insect treats, while cheerful zinnia and marigold, grown as annuals, produce abundant seeds. The fast-growing American sweetgum tree attracts insects to its flowers in the spring. In fall, it drops colorful, star-shaped leaves and a multitude of nutritional seeds.

HOW TO ATTRACT DARK-EYED JUNCOS

- Place a tray bird feeder low to the ground, and fill it with millet, corn, peanuts, or black-oil sunflower seeds.
- Plant shrubs for the birds to roost in and trees with dense foliage to give them cover from predators such as hawks.
- Allow a corner of your backyard to become a bit overgrown; unmowed grass produces plentiful seeds.

SUBSPECIES

Slate-colored Junco

FAVORITE FOODS

Seeds   Insects

Eastern Towhee

Pipilo erythrophthalmus

ORDER: Passeriformes | FAMILY: Emberizida

One of the largest species of sparrow residing in North America, the Eastern Towhee is often heard but rarely seen. The head and back of the male are black, as are the wings and tail, which bear white-tipped markings. Its underside is reddish brown with a white streak running down the middle; the female is similar, but her upper half is plain brown. The regional habitat can determine the color of the Eastern Towhee's eyes, which are either red or yellow. This sparrow finds its food either by foraging on the ground or rummaging in bushes and shrubs. The three-tone call of the Eastern Towhee has been interpreted as, "Drink Your Tea," a phrasing that gave it its name.

Male Eastern Towhee (adult)

Female Eastern Towhee

FOWL FACTS & FIGURES

LENGTH RANGE: 7–8 inches

WEIGHT: 1–1.8 ounces

WINGSPAN: 7.9–11 inches

SONG OR CALL: Song is whistlelike *drink your teee*. Call is *chewink*.

NEST: Cup-shaped nest of sticks, grass, bark, and other plant matter, lined with fine grass and animal hair, built on the ground beneath a bushy shrub or brush pile

EGGS:
Color: Cream or gray with dark speckles or spots
Incubation: 12–13 days
Clutch Size: 2–6 eggs

WHERE ARE THEY?

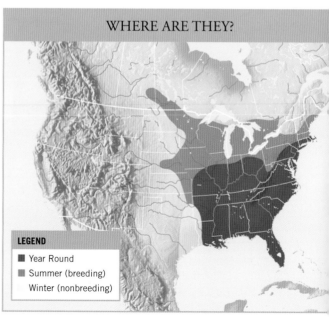

LEGEND
- Year Round
- Summer (breeding)
- Winter (nonbreeding)

BEST TREES AND PLANTS FOR YOUR GARDEN

❶ **Sassafras (genus *Sassafras*)** ❷ **Northern red oak (*Quercus borealis*)** ❸ **Arrowwood viburnum (*Viburnum dentatum*)** ❹ **Carpet bugle (*Ajuga reptans*):** A sassafras tree attracts many of the Eastern Towhee's favorite insects. The fragrant sassafras will provide your garden with richly colored autumn foliage. The northern red oak is a magnificent specimen tree that produces acorns—staples of the towhee diet. It also produces gold, russet, or scarlet foliage in the fall, making it a widely popular landscaping tree. Arrowwood viburnum is a hardy shrub that provides excellent cover. Carpet bugle will spread freely to create dense ground cover— an excellent hunting ground for the Eastern Towhee.

HOW TO ATTRACT EASTERN TOWHEES

Periwinkle

- Put out a tray feeder filled with millet seed.
- Plant ground-cover vegetation such as periwinkle *(Vinca minor)* or English ivy *(Hedera helix)*.
- Plant shrubs for roosting and foraging.

FAVORITE FOODS

Berries   Seeds   Acorns   Insects

Bobolink

Dolichonyx oryzivorus

ORDER: Passeriformes | FAMILY: Icterida

The male Bobolink is a unique specimen—the only North American bird with a black underside and lighter upperparts. During breeding season, the fluffy plumage of his shoulders and lower back is white, earning him the nickname "skunk blackbird." On his nape sits a tuft of creamy yellow feathers that look like a fuzzy blond toupee slipping from his head, which earns him another nickname: "butter bird." Yet another, "meadow-wink," pays tribute to this species' prairie home. The female has a yellow underside and brown upperparts with black streaks on the sides and back and under the tail. A black stripe extends from the eyes, and she has yellow and brown stripes on her head. The Bobolink's diet consists of seeds and small insects, but this bird also feeds on grains and rice which sometimes makes it a nuisance to farmers. Still, the Bobolink benefits many crops by eating harmful insects.

Male Bobolink (adult)

Female Bobolinks

FOWL FACTS & FIGURES

LENGTH RANGE: 6–8 inches

WEIGHT: 1–2 ounces

WINGSPAN: 10–12 inches

SONG OR CALL: Song is a bubbly series of notes and jangly tones. Call is a harsh *chek* or *pink*.

NEST: Simple nest made of dead grass and sedge, built on the ground

EGGS:
Color: Pale blue, gray, red, or brown with random brown splotches
Incubation: 11–13 days
Clutch Size: 1–7 eggs

WHERE ARE THEY?

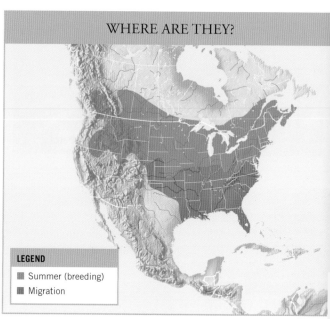

LEGEND
◼ Summer (breeding)
◼ Migration

BEST TREES AND PLANTS FOR YOUR GARDEN

❶ Silver mound artemisia (*Artemisia schmidtiana*)
❷ Switchgrass (*Panicum virgatum*) ❸ Big bluestem
(*Andropogon gerardii*) ❹ Indian blanket flower (*Gaillardia pulchella*) ❺ Azure sage (*Salvia azurea*): Surround a waving stand of ornamental grasses with silver mound artemisia to provide excellent foraging and a steady supply of seeds. The gray-green foliage of silver mound artemisia is an effective contrast to the red-purples of switchgrass in fall. A big bluestem cultivar, such as 'Big Daddy', is a sure lure to the meadow-loving Bobolink. This bluestem produces bright red seed heads and rich fall colors. A varied blend of annual flowers, including such species as Indian blanket flower, will create a seed-feeding wonderland for this bird. Indian blanket flower is also called firewheel—and for good reason. The red-orange petals fringed in amber yellow make this showy flower look like pinwheels on fire. A flowering perennial, such as azure sage, attracts seed eaters and makes a strong fall statement when its striking blue blooms first appear for their monthlong stay.

HOW TO ATTRACT BOBOLINKS

- Install a birdbath or fountain.
- Fill a tube feeder with sunflower seeds.
- Let a ditch get a bit overgrown; the ground-nesting Bobolink looks for protected depressions for its nest site.

FAVORITE FOODS

Grains   Seeds   Insects

Red-winged Blackbird

Agelaius phoeniceus

ORDER: Passeriformes | FAMILY: Icterida

Set up a backyard bird feeder, and this dramatic red-highlighted flier will come. The Red-winged Blackbird will eagerly indulge in almost any meal that can be found at a bird feeder, from seeds to fruit, but it can be a nuisance to farmers and gardeners alike. It is a territorial bird that will not hesitate to display aggression to any intruder, be it another bird or a human. The male is black with a vibrant red and yellow patch starting at the base of the wing. The female is a plain speckled brown bird that is smaller than the male. Male and female Red-winged Blackbirds migrate separately, but the male embarks earlier than the female so that he can establish his territory before the mating season begins. During the mating season, this polyamorous bird can amass a harem of up to 15 females.

Male Red-winged Blackbird (adult)

Female Red-winged Blackbird

FOWL FACTS & FIGURES

LENGTH RANGE: 7–9 inches

WEIGHT: 1–3 ounces

WINGSPAN: 12.2–15.7 inches

SONG OR CALL: Male's song is a pair of short, high-pitched notes. Females respond with a number of *chit* or *check* sounds. Call is a *check* or *chack*.

NEST: Cup-shaped nest tightly woven around supportive stems with an interior lined with wet leaves, mud, and grass; built low off the ground in shrubs or vegetation

EGGS:
Color: Pale blue, gray, and green with dark spots
Incubation: 11–13 days
Clutch Size: 2–4 eggs

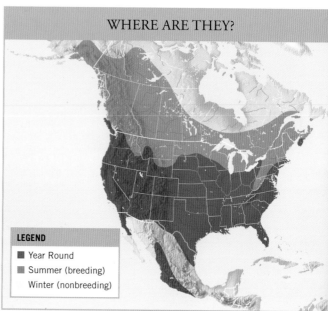

WHERE ARE THEY?

LEGEND
■ Year Round
■ Summer (breeding)
  Winter (nonbreeding)

BEST TREES AND PLANTS FOR YOUR GARDEN

❶ **Hawthorn (*Crataegus monogyna*) ❷ Callery pear (*Pyrus calleryana*) ❸ Black crowberry (*Empetrum nigrum*)**: The late-spring-blooming flowers of the hawthorn attract many insects. This plant can be grown as either a tree or a shrub; if grown as a shrub, it will also provide suitable nesting for the Red-winged Blackbird. In late spring, hawthorn comes alive with the red color of its fruit, known as haw. Birds eat these berries, and you can use them in jellies, jams, and syrups. Flowering trees, such as the Callery pear, attract insects and produce edible seeds. In spring, this hardy landscaping tree, also known as the Bradford pear, blooms in a riot of snowy blossoms. The evergreen crowberry thrives in soil that many other plants cannot tolerate, and it provides excellent ground cover for foraging birds, as well as edible fruit for birds and humans.

HOW TO ATTRACT RED-WINGED BLACKBIRDS

- Position a suet feeder low to the ground. Red-winged Blackbirds also eat weed seeds and nuisance insects.
- This bird often nests in a marsh or near a pond. You can simulate this environment by keeping your yard moist, especially during a dry spell. This has the added benefit of attracting the worms that this bird so enjoys.

FAVORITE FOODS

Seeds   **Grains**   **Insects**

Baltimore Oriole

Icterus galbula

The throaty whistle of the male Baltimore Oriole often gives away his presence before you see him—and he is a sight to behold. This small, distinctive bird has a bright orange underside that sharply contrasts with his deep black head. His back is black interspersed with white feathers that also extend down his black wings. The female is far less bold in coloration, with drab olive upperparts and a faded orange breast and belly. The Baltimore Oriole forages in trees or shrubs for its preferred diet of insects, berries, and nectars. It also snatches insects from the air during short feeding flights. This oriole's appetite for caterpillars helps protect woodlands from some destructive pests. It migrates south in the winter, but it will occasionally forgo migration if there is a regular food supply.

Male Baltimore Oriole (adult)

Juvenile (left) and female Baltimore Orioles feeding on jelly

FOWL FACTS & FIGURES

LENGTH RANGE: 6.5–7 inches

WEIGHT: 1–1.5 ounces

WINGSPAN: 11.25–12.5 inches

SONG OR CALL: Song is a simple series of whistles and chatter.

NEST: Bulbous nest woven from hair and various fibers suspended from tree branches

EGGS:
Color: Gray and white, marked with streaks and blotches, tapered at one end
Incubation: 11–14 days
Clutch Size: 3–7 eggs

WHERE ARE THEY?

LEGEND
- Summer (breeding)
- Winter (nonbreeding)
- Migration

BEST TREES AND PLANTS FOR YOUR GARDEN

❶ American sycamore (*Platanus occidentalis*) ❷ Eastern serviceberry (*Amelanchier canadensis*) ❸ Pin cherry (*Prunus pensylvanica*) ❹ Trumpet honeysuckle (*Lonicera sempervirens*): A safe nesting tree is an oriole draw. Although the Baltimore Oriole once used elms almost exclusively, these days it readily nests in other large deciduous trees, such as the American sycamore. Fruit trees, such as the eastern serviceberry, with its plump purple fruits, attract the Baltimore Oriole. Pin cherry is another oriole favorite. You can use the small red fruits of this tree to make jellies, jams, and preserves. To further indulge this bird's sweet tooth, plant a variety of nectar-producing flowers, such as trumpet honeysuckle. Not only will this coral stunner rival the Baltimore Oriole for color, if you let it flow over a fence or trellis, it can also stand up to the bird's weight as it sips nectar.

HOW TO ATTRACT BALTIMORE ORIOLES

- Create an oriole feeding station by adding fruits, such as grapes, oranges, apples, and cherries, to your tray bird feeder.
- Set out a saucer of grape jelly.
- Hang an oriole feeder filled with sugar water.

FAVORITE FOODS

Fruit

Nectar

Insects

Orchard Oriole

Icterus spurious

ORDER: Passeriformes | FAMILY: Icterida

A frequent visitor to suburban parks and backyards, this smallest member of the North American blackbird family sings a warbled, throaty song. The adult male has a chestnut-colored breast, rump, and shoulder. His head is black, and his wings are marked with white bars. The female's coloring has a different configuration: her back is olive green, and her belly is yellow. Her wings are dark brown, each with a thin white wing bar. The Orchard Oriole's favorite position for hunting is a perch on a low-hanging branch of a shade tree, where it feeds on a diet of insects and spiders. Like other orioles, the Orchard Oriole will also collect nectar from certain flowers.

Male Orchard Oriole (adult)

Female Orchard Oriole

FOWL FACTS & FIGURES

LENGTH RANGE: 6–7 inches

WEIGHT: 0.5–1 ounce

WINGSPAN: 9.25–10.25 inches

SONG OR CALL: Song is an unpredictable combination of whistled notes. Call consists of *chucks* and chatter.

NEST: Cup-shaped, woven from grass, feathers, and wool; found on the ends of tree branches

EGGS:

Color: Light blue with dark spots

Incubation: 12–14 days

Clutch Size: 3–7 eggs

WHERE ARE THEY?

LEGEND

■ Summer (breeding)
　Winter (nonbreeding)
▩ Migration

BEST TREES AND PLANTS FOR YOUR GARDEN

❶ **Eastern cottonwood** (*Populus deltoides*) ❷ **Desert willow** (*Chilopsis linearis*) ❸ **Black cherry** (*Prunus serotina*) ❹ **Hollyhock** (*Alcea rosea*): A large shade tree like the eastern cottonwood is an excellent nesting habitat for the Orchard Oriole. This tree gets its name from its cottony, seed-rich catkins. The nectar of the desert willow is a sweet treat for the Orchard Oriole, and the red, pink, or purple flowers it produces in late spring bring a garden alive. The astringent fruit of the black cherry tree is a favorite of orioles and many other birds. To add rich color and quench this bird's craving for nectar, add a grouping of hollyhock to your garden. The saucer-shaped flowers of this plant twirl up the tall stems, which can reach from 5 to 8 feet high. These yellow, red, purple, pink, or white blooms begin in midsummer and last about two months.

HOW TO ATTRACT ORCHARD ORIOLES

- Plant nectar-producing flowers—they also attract insects that the Orchard Oriole will eat.
- Hang a jelly bird feeder in your yard.
- Add a variety of fruits, including oranges, raisins, and apple slices, to your tray bird feeder.

FAVORITE FOODS

Spiders **Nectar** **Fruit** **Insects**

Western Meadowlark

Archilochus alexandri

ORDER: Passeriformes | FAMILY: Icterida

This large, stout songbird has a long, thin beak and a short tail. The male and female Western Meadowlark differ only slightly, most notably in size, with the male measuring a little bigger than the female. The neck and underside of both male and female are bright yellow, with a distinctive black V-shaped marking below the throat and a black and brown pattern on the crown. It has a brown upper body and white flanks; black markings speckle both The mating ritual of this songbird consists of a dramatic chase as the male bird pursues its mate—or mates, because a male Western Meadowlark usually has two breeding partners. Its melodious song has a flutelike quality.

Western
Meadowlark
(adult)

Western Meadowlark foraging through grassland

FOWL FACTS & FIGURES

LENGTH RANGE: 6–10 inches

WEIGHT: 3–4 ounces

WINGSPAN: 14–16 inches

SONG OR CALL: Song is a slow, flutelike, deep whistle. Call is a distinctive *chupp* sound.

NEST: Cup made from bark and dried grass, usually partially covered and found on the ground, hidden among surrounding plants

EGGS:
Color: Pale pink speckled in purple-brown
Incubation: 13–15 days
Clutch Size: 3–6 eggs

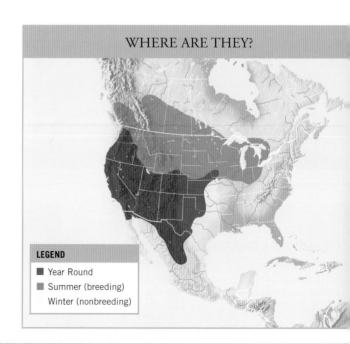

WHERE ARE THEY?

LEGEND
- Year Round
- Summer (breeding)
- Winter (nonbreeding)

BEST TREES AND PLANTS FOR YOUR GARDEN

❶ Western serviceberry (*Amelanchier alnifolia*) **❷** California oat grass (*Danthonia californica*) **❸** Switchgrass (*Panicum virgatum*) **❹** Red fescue (*Festuca rubra*) **❺** Plains coreopsis (*Coreopsis tinctoria*): As its name suggest, this bird is a creature of meadows and prairies. If you have space, create a grassland habitat on your property to lure the Western Meadowlark. Look for a varied selection of native or noninvasive grasses, shrubs, and flowers that are easy to maintain. For dry to moist areas, the berry-producing western serviceberry works well. Spiky California oat grass will work well in moist areas. When its seeds ripen, switchgrass can take on a pinkish tone. This grass attracts a variety of insects, including caterpillars and grasshoppers. Red fescue—actually a dark green—produces a prairie effect when left unmowed. Add lots of seed-producing annuals, such as the plains coreopsis, to brighten your meadow landscape. A dark maroon-brown center highlights the bright red and yellow petals of this charming flower.

HOW TO ATTRACT WESTERN MEADOWLARKS

- Leave a fence post or tree stump standing to provide this singer with a perch.
- Allow a corner of your property to become a bit overgrown—the Western Meadowlark likes to forage in underbrush.

FAVORITE FOODS

Grains   Seeds   Insects

American Goldfinch

Carduelis tristis

ORDER: Passeriformes | FAMILY: Fringillid[a]

The American Goldfinch is a stunning songbird of the finch family. The male has bright yellow plumage, and his wings are detailed with black-and-white edging. The female's plumage is a comparatively dull yellow tinged with olive green. An interesting trait of the male American Goldfinch is that he molts prior to the breeding season; the new feathers that grow back are of an even more intense and striking shade of yellow. Its diet consists mainly of seeds and grains. The American Goldfinch is a very social bird that often travels in flocks. Although generally not aggressive, it will defend its nest if threatened. It has an energetic, undulating flight pattern, and it often calls whi[le] in flight. Its beautiful song, which earned it the nickname "wild canary," is a melodic series of twittering warbles.

American Goldfinch (adult)

Female Goldfinch

FOWL FACTS & FIGURES

LENGTH RANGE: 4–5 inches

WEIGHT: 0.4–0.7 ounce

WINGSPAN: 7–9 inches

SONG OR CALL: Song is a rapid, random series of excited notes. Calls vary from the quiet, even-cadenced contact call that sounds like *po-ta-to-chip* to an excited *tee-yee* courtship call from the male.

NEST: Cup made from bark and dried grass, usually partially covered and found on the ground, hidden among surrounding plants

EGGS:

Color: Pale blue and white, occasionally with brown spots

Incubation: 12–17 days

Clutch Size: 2–7 eggs

WHERE ARE THEY?

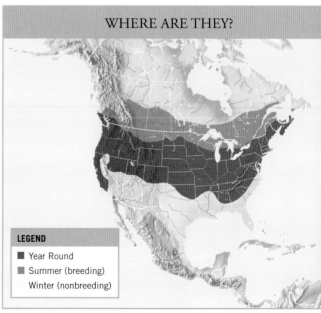

LEGEND

■ Year Round
■ Summer (breeding)
　 Winter (nonbreeding)

BEST TREES AND PLANTS FOR YOUR GARDEN

❶ Japanese maple (*Acer palmatum*) ❷ Sunflower (*Helianthus annuus*) ❸ New England aster (*Aster novae-angliae*) ❹ Red mulberry (*Morus rubra*): In mid- to late summer, the American Goldfinch finds a young tree an ideal place to roost. A Japanese maple also provides it with edible seeds. With its dramatic, twisted dark limbs and bright red leaves, this tree is a landscaper's favorite. Finches love sunflower seeds, so you can't go wrong planting a cluster of these annuals. The thistles so loved by finches tend to be too invasive for a backyard garden, but there are many flowers that produce abundant seeds that will attract the American Goldfinch. The New England aster, like thistles, is a member of the Asteraceae family, but this perennial is a great garden addition. With yellow discs surrounded by lilac to blue-purple petals, the blooms add color to a fall garden. When other food is scarce, the American Goldfinch relies on berries, such as deep purple-blue mulberries.

HOW TO ATTRACT GOLDFINCHES

- Hang a niger feeder in your yard, and put out a tray feeder filled with black-oil sunflower seeds.
- Fill a birdbath with a fresh supply of water for a sip or a dip.
- Sprinkle some rock salt on a saucer.

FAVORITE FOODS

Berries   **Seeds**   **Insects**

House Finch

Carpodacus mexicanus

ORDER: Passeriformes | FAMILY: Fringillida

The aptly named House Finch is a gregarious bird that lives in harmony with the human race, whether nibbling at a backyard bird feeder or making its nest in a hanging plant on a porch. It gets its name from its habit of nesting under house eaves, but it also nests in trees and shrubs. Its plumage is brownish gray to salt and pepper, with streaked patterns on its underside, wings, and tail. Red highlights throughout the head, breast, and rump are exclusive to the male House Finch and can, on rare occasions, change according to his diet. The ingestion of certain fruits and berries will change his pigmentation to yellow or orange. The female is a plain, brown-speckled bird. The House Finch's preferred diet works well for gardeners: it eats mostly grains, seeds, and berries, and voraciously devours the seeds of pesky weeds like dandelio and nettle, along with the aphids that cling to them.

Male House Finch (adult)

Female House Finch

FOWL FACTS & FIGURES

LENGTH RANGE: 5–5.5 inches

WEIGHT: 0.5–1 ounce

WINGSPAN: 8–10 inches

SONG OR CALL: Male's song is marked by a distinctive upward or downward note, slurred at the end. Males and females call with an insistent *chee-eep.*

NEST: Cup-shaped, crafted from assorted leaves and twigs as well as feathers and soft natural materials, and found in trees, as well as on top of buildings, ledges, and hanging surfaces/structures.

EGGS:
Color: Light blue and white, with black and purple specks
Incubation: 13–14 days
Clutch Size: 2–6 eggs

WHERE ARE THEY?

LEGEND
■ Year Round

BEST TREES AND PLANTS FOR YOUR GARDEN

❶ Norway spruce (*Picea abies*) ❷ American beautyberry
(*Callicarpa americana*) ❸ Gerbera (genus *Gerbera*)
❹ Compass flower (*Silphium laciniatum*): The House Finch
will appreciate an evergreen, such as a spruce, for cover and a place
to perch. The densely clustered fruit of the American beautyberry
is worthy of this plant's common name. Not only beautiful, these
intense purple berries lure many birds, including the House Finch.
Ensure a steady diet of seeds, and this bird will regularly visit. The
neon-bright gerbera and the sunflowerlike compass flower, with
their sought-after thistlelike seeds, are just two of the many colorful
members of the Asteraceae family that attract many finches.

HOW TO ATTRACT HOUSE FINCHES

- Hang a niger feeder in your garden.
- Put out a tray or platform feeder filled with
  black-oil sunflower seeds and peanuts.
- Toss bread or cracker crumbs into your yard.
  House Finches love baked goods!

FAVORITE FOODS

Buds   Seeds   Fruit

Pine Siskin

Carduelis pinus

ORDER: Passeriformes | FAMILY: Fringillidae

This gregarious small finch has a fairly muted appearance. The adult male and the adult female have brown backs and grayish white undersides with wings accented with darker streaks. Yellow patches highlight the wings and notched tail. These patches tend to be more noticeable on the male. A very social bird, the Pine Siskin prefers the company of other siskins and finches and nests in loose colonies. It does not typically migrate in the winter unless there is an imbalance or shortage of the food supply in its resident area. When migration does occur, the Pine Siskin travels in a flock. The diet of this bird consists of plants, seeds, and insects, and it will eat readily from a seed feeder.

**Male
Pine Siskin
(adult)**

Female Pine Siskin

FOWL FACTS & FIGURES

LENGTH RANGE: 4–5.5 inches

WEIGHT: 0.4–0.6 ounce

WINGSPAN: 7–9 inches

SONG OR CALL: Call is an unusual, metallic zipping chatter.

NEST: Shallow, soft lining, usually well-hidden near the ends of upper tree branches

EGGS:
Color: Light blue and green with brown spots on the larger end
Incubation: 13 days
Clutch Size: 1–6 eggs

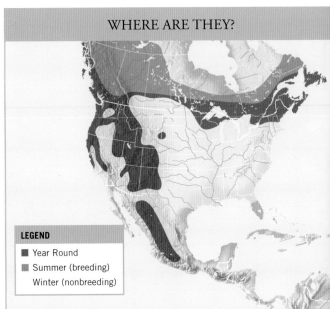

WHERE ARE THEY?

LEGEND
■ Year Round
■ Summer (breeding)
　 Winter (nonbreeding)

BEST TREES AND PLANTS FOR YOUR GARDEN

❶ **Arborvitae (genus *Thuja*)** ❷ **Larch (genus *Larix*)** ❸ **Birch (genus *Betula*)** ❹ **Sunflower (*Helianthus annuus*)**: The dense, thick canopy of the cone-shaped evergreen arborvitae makes a secure place for the conifer-loving Pine Siskin to nest. The larch tree is valued for its color and variety; its needlelike leaves change color in the autumn before dropping completely in winter. Birch trees have extremely resilient bark and come in a variety of shades ranging between yellow, silver, red, black, and white. The Pine Siskin enjoys sunflower seeds, as do other finches, so find a spot for this flower.

HOW TO ATTRACT PINE SISKINS

- Hang a tubular bird feeder in your yard, and keep it filled with black-oil sunflower seeds. The Pine Siskin also enjoys eating from a hanging peanut feeder.
- Introduce shrubs for foraging.
- Install a birdbath in your garden.

FAVORITE FOODS

Conifer Seeds   **Seeds**   **Insects**

Red Crossbill

Loxia curvirostra

ORDER: Passeriformes | FAMILY: Fringillidae

This breed is named for the pronounced crisscrossing of its mandibles. The male has predominately rusty red plumage with dark brown markings on its crown and near the eyes. The female has greenish yellow plumage. Both sexes share the same long, pointed wings in smoky grayish brown, but the male's wings tend to be a slightly darker shade. Hatched with a straight beak, a young crossbill will develop its unique bill by the time it is about 45 days old.

The beak's scissorlike shape enables this finch to gain access to the seeds inside conifer cones, which are the main source of its diet. To pry the seeds from a cone, it holds the cone with one foot, inserts its closed bill between the cone and the scales, and then opens its bill. It can then extract the seeds with its flexible tongue. The Red Crossbill will mate throughout the year, as long as there is a sufficient supply of food nearby.

Male Red Crossbill (adult)

Female Red Crossbill

FOWL FACTS & FIGURES

LENGTH RANGE: 5.5–8 inches

WEIGHT: 0.8–1.6 ounces

WINGSPAN: 10–11 inches

SONG OR CALL: Song is an extremely concise pairing of whistles and clicks. Call is a similar, short *cheep*.

NEST: Cup-shaped, made of twigs with a lining of various fibers, needles, and grass, and usually well hidden in trees among branches and leaves.

EGGS:
Color: White with red marks and streaks
Incubation: 11–14 days
Clutch Size: 2–6 eggs

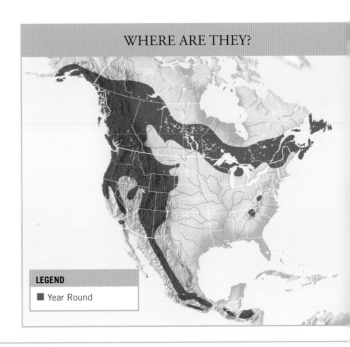

WHERE ARE THEY?

LEGEND
■ Year Round

BEST TREES AND PLANTS FOR YOUR GARDEN

❶ Douglas fir (*Pseudotsuga menziesii*) ❷ Eastern hemlock (*Tsuga canadensis*) ❸ Ponderosa pine (*Pinus ponderosa*):
The Red Crossbill depends on conifer seeds, such as those produced by spruces. Douglas fir also produces seed-rich cones that this bird thrives on. The feathery, graceful eastern hemlock is another welcome landscaping choice. This fast-growing conifer is primarily valued for its rich seed output, but it also provides a suitable place for the Red Crossbill to nest. Many pine species are crossbill favorites, and if you are lucky enough to have mature trees, such as a stand of ponderosa pine, this bird will feast on the cones' seeds.

HOW TO ATTRACT RED CROSSBILLS

- Install a birdbath or fountain in your garden or backyard.
- Hang a tube feeder filled with safflower seeds and millet.
- Add peanuts, apple slices, and other pieces of fruit to a tray feeder.

FAVORITE FOODS

Conifer Seeds	Seeds	Insects

73

Northern Cardinal

Cardinalis cardinalis

ORDER: Passeriformes | FAMILY: Cardinalidae

The Northern Cardinal is really a bird of eastern North America, where it thrives in gardens, parks, and woodlands. This premier member of the Cardinal family is best known for the male's rich red plumage, the distinctive spiked tuft on his crown, and his black face markings. The female is dull, almost brown, with rosy tones that are most pronounced in the wing, tail, and crest feathers. She has comparatively drab face markings and a red-orange bill.

This species mates for life and stays paired year-round. It forages on the ground, hopping from place to place in search of seeds, grass, grains, and fruit, but its diet also includes insects, such as beetles and caterpillars. The Northern Cardinal is a territorial songbird, the male calling to mark and defend his territory. Human actions, such as providing feeders and creating welcoming garden habitats, have contributed to the increased numbers of this bird.

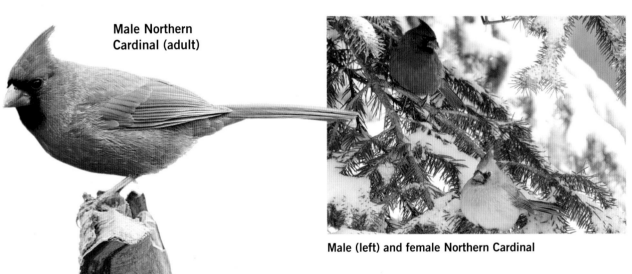

Male Northern Cardinal (adult)

Male (left) and female Northern Cardinal

FOWL FACTS & FIGURES

LENGTH RANGE: 8–9 inches

WEIGHT: 1.5–1.7 ounces

WINGSPAN: 10–12 inches

SONG OR CALL: Sings a series of paired, whistled notes. Call consists of a short, sharp *chip*.

NEST: Cup-shaped, layered with twigs, trash, bark, grass, and stems, and usually hidden in branches, shrubs, or vines

EGGS:

Color: Drab gray or buff, occasionally white or light green, with gray and brown specks

Incubation: 11–13 days

Clutch Size: 2–5 eggs

WHERE ARE THEY?

LEGEND

■ Year Round

BEST TREES AND PLANTS FOR YOUR GARDEN

❶ Cherry plum (*Prunus cerasifera*) ❷ Apple (*Malus domestica*) ❸ Snowball tree (*Viburnum opulus*) ❹ Chinese juniper (*Juniperus chinensis*): The delicate flowers of a small cherry plum tree are springtime stunners. As summer advances, the cherry plums ripen to provide an abundant source of nutrition for the Northern Cardinal. An orchard apple tree also produces lovely white blossoms in spring. In fall, any one of the hundreds of varieties of apple tree will produce delicious fruit. The red berries of the snowball tree also attract the Northern Cardinal. In spring and summer, this viburnum bursts into bloom with showy globes of lace-capped flowers that range in color from pale green to creamy white. To ensure that this year-round resident has shelter in the winter months, plant evergreen trees and shrubs, such as Chinese juniper.

HOW TO ATTRACT NORTHERN CARDINALS

- Fill a feeder with black-oil sunflower seeds, cracked corn, safflower seeds, and, for a special treat, peanuts.
- Introduce evergreen trees and shrubs for nesting and roosting.
- Install a year-round heated birdbath.

FAVORITE FOODS

Berries   **Fruit**   **Seeds**   **Insects**

Summer Tanager

Piranga rubra

ORDER: Passeriformes | FAMILY: Cardinalida

This eye-catching songbird is red with darker and lighter shades blended throughout its plumage. The female of the species is a mixture of orange and mustard yellow. The Summer Tanager is a formidable exterminator of bees and wasps: it strikes in flight and rarely misses its target. It feeds heavily during the summer, storing fat for its long migration—a journey that can span more than 50 miles. This bird sings a pleasant melody of several clearly phrased notes. The song closely resembles, and is easily mistaken for, the song of the American Robin.

Male Summer Tanager (adult)

Female Summer Tanager

FOWL FACTS & FIGURES

LENGTH RANGE: 6.5–7 inches

WEIGHT: 1–1.5 ounces

WINGSPAN: 11–12 inches

SONG OR CALL: A repeating, slurred whistle. The call is a simple trio of *click* or *cluck* sounds.

NEST: Simple, cup-shaped, found in leaves or among hanging, horizontal branches

EGGS:

Color: Light blue and green with dark markings

Incubation: 11–12 days

Clutch Size: 2–5 eggs

WHERE ARE THEY?

LEGEND

■ Summer (breeding)

□ Winter (nonbreeding)

■ Migration

BEST TREES AND PLANTS FOR YOUR GARDEN

❶ Blazing star (*Liatris spicata*) ❷ Flowering dogwood (*Cornus florida*) ❸ Apple (*Malus domestica*): To satisfy the Summer Tanager's hunger for bees and wasps, choose plants that attract these insects. The wispy blooms of blazing star are bee magnets. This perennial, known for its showy purple to pale pink flowers, blooms in July and August. It can reach a height of 4 feet. Bees like trees, too, including the flowering dogwood. It offers the Summer Tanager shelter and fruit, as well as insect-attracting flowers. Orchard trees, such as apple, will give this bird a winter source of fruit.

HOW TO ATTRACT SUMMER TANAGERS

- Attach a tray feeder to a freestanding post, and fill it with fruits.
- Install a birdbath, fountain, or other water feature.
- Plant insect-attracting plants, such as clover (genus *Trifolium*), in your yard. The insects that come to these plants will consume other, parasitic insects, as well as attract the Summer Tanager.

FAVORITE FOODS

Insects

Fruit

Indigo Bunting

Passerina amoena

ORDER: Passeriformes | FAMILY: Cardinalid∶

The gorgeous color that gives the Indigo Bunting its name is only seen during mating season, when the male displays iridescent blue plumage to attract a mate. In winter, most of the male's feathers dull to a brown shade that resembles the coloration of the female. The female has a brown back with a tan underside and black tips on her tail and wings. As with the feathers of the commonly seen Blue Jay, it is light refraction that makes the feathers of th male Indigo Bunting appear blue; in low light, they look blackish. The Indigo Bunting is an adaptable eater and enjoys a varied diet. It consumes weed seeds, insects, and other pests, making it helpful to farmers and gardeners. It will migrate during the winter, setting off after sunset and using the stars as guides as it flies by night.

Male Indigo Bunting (adult)

Female Indigo Bunting

FOWL FACTS & FIGURES

LENGTH RANGE: 4.5–5 inches

WEIGHT: 0.4–0.6 ounce

WINGSPAN: 8–9 inches

SONG OR CALL: Sings a long, melodic phrase. Calls with a succinct *spit* sound.

NEST: Cup-shaped, woven from leaves and grass, lined with grass and hair bound with spider webbing; found near the ground in a shrub or other foliage

EGGS:

Color: White, occasionally with brown spots

Incubation: 11–14 days

Clutch Size: 1–4 eggs

WHERE ARE THEY?

LEGEND

■ Summer (breeding)

Winter (nonbreeding)

▥ Migration

BEST TREES AND PLANTS FOR YOUR GARDEN

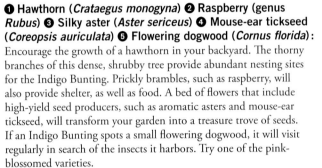

❶ Hawthorn (*Crataegus monogyna*) ❷ Raspberry (genus *Rubus*) ❸ Silky aster (*Aster sericeus*) ❹ Mouse-ear tickseed (*Coreopsis auriculata*) ❺ Flowering dogwood (*Cornus florida*):
Encourage the growth of a hawthorn in your backyard. The thorny branches of this dense, shrubby tree provide abundant nesting sites for the Indigo Bunting. Prickly brambles, such as raspberry, will also provide shelter, as well as food. A bed of flowers that include high-yield seed producers, such as aromatic asters and mouse-ear tickseed, will transform your garden into a treasure trove of seeds. If an Indigo Bunting spots a small flowering dogwood, it will visit regularly in search of the insects it harbors. Try one of the pink-blossomed varieties.

HOW TO ATTRACT INDIGO BUNTINGS

- Hang a feeder, and fill with niger seeds.
- Plant short trees or shrubs with thick limbs for foraging and roosting.
- Create a small vegetable patch. These birds especially enjoy lettuce seeds.

FAVORITE FOODS

Berries **Nuts** **Seeds** **Insects**

Black-headed Grosbeak

Pheucticus melanocephalus

ORDER: Passeriformes | FAMILY: Cardinalida

The head, wings, and tail of this grosbeak are black interspersed with white patches; the rest of its body is a ginger hue. The female Black-headed Grosbeak has duller plumage than the male, and her feathers are brown in places where his are black. The male's distinctive song, which he usually delivers from a prominent perch, sounds like a scale of notes played on a flute. The female sings a similar song but leaves out certain notes. During the breeding season, the male and female share incubating and feeding duties. The female, however, plays a cunning trick on her mate that helps to ensure that he takes on his full share of chores: she sings the male version of the Black-headed Grosbeak song, which compels him to stay with their eggs out of concern that another male is on the prow

Male Black-headed Grosbeak (adult)

Female Black-headed Grosbeak

FOWL FACTS & FIGURES

LENGTH RANGE: 7–7.5 inches

WEIGHT: 1–1.7 ounces

WINGSPAN: 12–12.5 inches

SONG OR CALL: Song is a series of alternating high and low notes. Call is a *chink*.

NEST: Cup-shaped, loosely woven from twigs, stems, and pine needles, found in trees and shrubs, often near water

EGGS:

Color: Light blue and green with brown and red spots, tapered on the light end

Incubation: 12–14 days

Clutch Size: 2–5 eggs

WHERE ARE THEY?

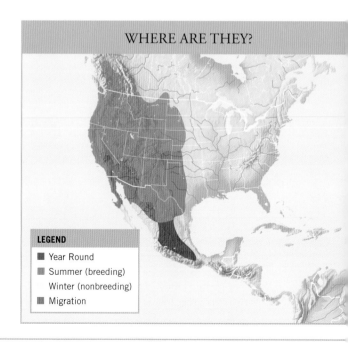

LEGEND
- Year Round
- Summer (breeding)
- Winter (nonbreeding)
- Migration

BEST TREES AND PLANTS FOR YOUR GARDEN

❶ **Arrowwood viburnum** (*Viburnum dentatum*) ❷ **Pine (genus** *Pinus*) ❸ **Box elder** (*Acer negundo*) ❹ **Cockspur hawthorn** (*Crataegus crus-galli*): Arrowhead viburnum is a dense shrub that offers many appealing amenities to a Black-headed Grosbeak. It produces a crop of small blue berries in late summer and continues to bear fruit throughout the fall. It also provides good cover for foraging or nesting. Pine and box elder trees are also excellent places to forage and nest. The cockspur hawthorn can be grown either as a small tree or as a shrub. Its flowers bloom in the spring, and its berries start to ripen at the end of the summer, providing sustenance for the Black-headed Grosbeak that continues into midwinter.

HOW TO ATTRACT BLACK-HEADED GROSBEAKS

- Offer black-oil sunflower seeds in a hopper feeder that has ample perching space for grosbeak visitors.
- Hang a suet bird feeder in your yard as an additional attraction.

FAVORITE FOODS

Insects   Seeds   Fruit

Rose-breasted Grosbeak

Pheucticus ludovicianus

ORDER: Passeriformes | FAMILY: Cardinalid

A member of the cardinal family, the Rose-breasted Grosbeak has black feathers on its back and a white underside. Its wings are black with white markings concealing red feathers underneath. A vivid splash of deep rose-red marks its chest. The female has much less vibrant plumage than her counterpart, and hers is speckled where his is solid. The call of the Rose-breasted Grosbeak is similar to that of a robin, but it is more harmonious and graceful. Its diet consists primarily of insects, seeds, and berries, most of which it gleans from trees. This bird winters in Mexico and Central America but returns to North America for the breeding season.

Male Rose-breasted Grosbeak (adult)

Female Rose-breasted Grosbeak

FOWL FACTS & FIGURES

LENGTH RANGE: 7–8.5 inches

WEIGHT: 1.4–1.7 ounces

WINGSPAN: 11.4–13 inches

SONG OR CALL: Song is a musical series of slow, low notes. Call is either a *squeak* or a *squawk*.

NEST: Cup-shaped, loosely woven, and often lined with hair, found in shrubs, trees, and vines

EGGS:

Color: Light blue or green with brown or red specks

Incubation: 13–14 days

Clutch Size: 1–5 eggs

WHERE ARE THEY?

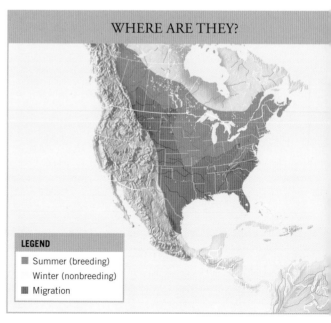

LEGEND

■ Summer (breeding)

Winter (nonbreeding)

▥ Migration

BEST TREES AND PLANTS FOR YOUR GARDEN

❶ Pagoda dogwood (*Cornus alternifolia*) ❷ Black tupelo (*Nyssa sylvatica*) ❸ American red elder (*Sambucus pubens*):
The horizontal growth pattern that lends this ornamental shrub a pagoda-like appearance gives the pagoda dogwood its name. In summer, clusters of small white flowers appear. By late summer, its blue-black fruits begin luring birds. The Rose-breasted Grosbeak will also use its branches for shelter and nesting. The black tupelo is also a grosbeak favorite. As well as providing a sheltering site, in September it produces tempting bluish black drupes. This tall tree is a great yard addition, with showy florescent yellow to orange to red or purple fall foliage. The American red elder attracts many birds, and its glistening red berries ripen just when baby birds need them in midsummer. Soon after ripening, elderberries usually disappear— grosbeaks and other fruit-eating birds strip the shrub's branches bare.

HOW TO ATTRACT ROSE-BREASTED GROSBEAKS

- Put out a hopper bird feeder filled with black-oil sunflower seeds.
- Plant low-growing shrubs and small trees to provide plentiful foraging opportunities for the grosbeak.

FAVORITE FOODS

Berries   Spiders   Seeds   Insects

Blue Grosbeak

Passerina caerulea

ORDER: Passeriformes | FAMILY: Cardinalida

The male Blue Grosbeak may be one of the prettiest backyard birds in North America, yet it is rarely seen. Its plumage is a sight to behold: the back feathers of the male are brilliant blue with black and chestnut hues mixed throughout the wings. A black ring encircles the eyes and extends to the base of the beak, which shimmers with silver. The female is predominately brown with some blue feathers on her back. Her wings are dark brown to black with brown wing bars and edging. The diet of the Blue Grosbeak consists of a wide range of insects, fruits, and grains, and it will readily forage for food in trees and on the ground. The song of the Blue Grosbeak is long and harmonic, and its call tends to resemble the sound of an insect more than of a bird.

Male Blue Grosbeak (adult)

Female (left) and male Blue Grosbeak

FOWL FACTS & FIGURES

LENGTH RANGE: 6–6.3 inches

WEIGHT: 0.9–1.1 ounces

WINGSPAN: 11 inches

SONG OR CALL: Song is a warbly assortment of short notes. Call is either a *buzz* or *tink*.

NEST: Small, cup-shaped, usually found in shrubs or small trees

EGGS:

Color: Light blue

Incubation: 11–12 days

Clutch Size: 3–5 eggs

WHERE ARE THEY?

LEGEND

- Year Round
- Summer (breeding)
- Winter (nonbreeding)
- Migration

BEST TREES AND PLANTS FOR YOUR GARDEN

❶ Common juniper (*Juniperus communis*) ❷ Himalayan knotweed (*Persicaria affinis*) ❸ Buffaloberry (*Shepherdia argentea*) ❹ Red mulberry (*Morus rubra*): Common juniper is a dense spreading shrub that offers the Blue Grosbeak a great place to nest. It also attracts scores of insects. In the fall, juniper produces tiny dark blue berries that the Blue Grosbeak enjoys. The bicolored perennial Himalayan knotweed also attracts a variety of insects and provides excellent ground cover and foraging space. The Blue Grosbeak likes the summer-ripening, bright red fruit of the buffaloberry, which is a large shrub. A red mulberry tree produces sweet, edible berries that birds—and humans—devour. These berries make great jams, jellies, and preserves.

HOW TO ATTRACT BLUE GROSBEAKS

- Install a fountain or a birdbath in your yard.
- Put out a hopper bird feeder filled with black-oil sunflower seeds, millet, and corn.
- Hang or mount a tray bird feeder filled with assorted dried fruits.

FAVORITE FOODS

Buds	Fruit	Seeds	Insects

Gray Catbird

Dumetella carolinensis

ORDER: Passeriformes | FAMILY: Mimid

This bird is named for its distinctive call, which is similar to a cat's *mew*. It also has the ability to mimic the sounds of other birds and tree frogs. The Gray Catbird enjoys a quiet, secluded habitat deep within foliage or beside a body of water, and it prefers to sing while concealed within the leaves of a tree or bush. Its plumage is solid dark gray, and it has a dark cap and bill. Its tail is long, and there is usually a reddish patch of color on the underside. The Gray Catbird will eat a diet of small insec that live in the ground, as well as a variety of berries.

Gray Catbird (adult)

Gray Catbird showing orange tail feathers

FOWL FACTS & FIGURES

LENGTH RANGE: 8–9.5 inches

WEIGHT: 0.8–2 ounces

WINGSPAN: 9–10 inches

SONG OR CALL: Song is lengthy, random, and often includes imitated notes or sounds from the surrounding environment. Call is a squawking *mew* reminiscent of a cat's meow.

NEST: Bulky, cup-shaped, made from mud, trash, and twigs; well-hidden deep within tree branches

EGGS:

Color: Light green or turquoise, occasionally with red specks

Incubation: 12–15 days

Clutch Size: 1–6 eggs

WHERE ARE THEY?

LEGEND

■ Year Round
■ Summer (breeding)
  Winter (nonbreeding)
■ Migration

BEST TREES AND PLANTS FOR YOUR GARDEN

❶ American beautyberry (*Callicarpa americana*) ❷ Barberry (genus *Berberis*) ❸ Black chokeberry (*Aronia melanocarpa*) ❹ Winterberry (*Ilex verticillata*): American beautyberry is a shrub with a lot of visual appeal. Its clustering flowers bloom in a range of colors from pink to blue. The small purple berries that continue to grow well into winter are an important staple of the Gray Catbird's diet. A dense shrub, such as barberry, will give these birds a great place to nest and will provide plentiful fruit. Black chokeberry, another bird-pleasing berry producer, looks great in fall, with its slim red leaves offsetting the dark, almost black, berries. Planting at least one member of the genus *Ilex* is a surefire way to lure scores of birds, including the Gray Catbird, to your garden. Winterberry is a particularly pretty species, with dark green foliage that contrasts with the orange-red fruit that appears in fall and lasts all winter long.

HOW TO ATTRACT GRAY CATBIRDS

- The Gray Catbird loves to bathe, so install a small birdbath or a pond in your backyard.
- Encourage ground cover for insect foraging.
- Fill a tray feeder or a plate with an offering of apples, grape jelly, and raisins.

FAVORITE FOODS

Insects

Berries

Fruit

Northern Mockingbird

Mimus polyglottos

ORDER: Passeriformes | FAMILY: Mimid

The slender Northern Mockingbird has a gray upper body and an almost white underside. Its tail is long and narrow, and it has a thin beak. The male and female look alike. The Northern Mockingbird often spreads its wings to flash its brighter underside. The reason for this common display is unknown, but many ornithologists believe that it is a hunting ritual, which either startles or lures insects into the open for the bird to prey on. The Northern Mockingbird's diet ranges from insects and fruit to spiders, snails, and small snakes. This bird loves to sing, and it does so often and loudly, by day and night (especially during a full moon). It is famed for its talents in mimicry—it can imitate not just the calls and songs of other birds but just about any other sound it hears, as wel

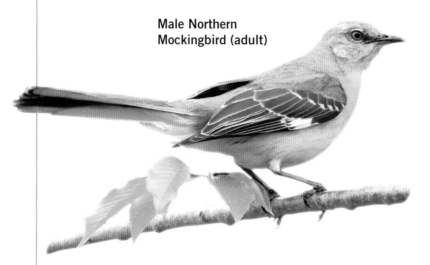

Male Northern Mockingbird (adult)

Fledgling Northern Mockingbird

FOWL FACTS & FIGURES

LENGTH RANGE: 8–10.5 inches

WEIGHT: 1.5–2 ounces

WINGSPAN: 13–15 inches

SONG OR CALL: Song consists of whistles and learned sounds imitative of those made by other birds and wildlife. Call is a harsh *chew* or *chat*, usually provoked by danger.

NEST: Cup-shaped, built from dead twigs, lined with grasses and random trash

EGGS:

Color: Light blue or green, with brown or red marks

Incubation: 12–13 days

Clutch Size: 2–6 eggs

WHERE ARE THEY?

LEGEND
- Year Round
- Summer (breeding)

BEST TREES AND PLANTS FOR YOUR GARDEN

❶ Northern bayberry (*Myrica pensylvanica*) ❷ Eastern redcedar (*Juniperus virginiana*) ❸ Eastern arborvitae (*Thuja occidentalis*) ❹ Sugar maple (*Acer saccharum*): The Northern Mockingbird readily eats the fruit of the northern bayberry. A highly aromatic pale grayish lavender wax covers the skin of bayberries. This wax, used in candle making, burns with a pleasing fragrance often associated with the holiday season. The blue berries of the Eastern redcedar, which are also waxy, are important winter foods for many birds. The eastern arborvitae is a small evergreen tree that makes an excellent hedge for a garden or yard. This shrubby tree also provides the Northern Mockingbird with an ideal nesting site. Another mockingbird favorite is the sugar maple, prized for its sweet sap.

HOW TO ATTRACT NORTHERN MOCKINGBIRDS

- Plant an assortment of berry-producing shrubs and trees.
- Encourage ground cover for foraging.
- Put out a tray bird feeder filled with a combination of seeds and fruit.

FAVORITE FOODS

| Berries | Fruit | Spiders | Insects |

Yellow Warbler

Dendroica petechia

ORDER: Passeriformes | FAMILY: Mimidae

A descendant of one of the many subspecies of American Warbler, this small bird is one of the most vibrant yellow birds in North America. The male is predominantly bright gold with a greenish yellow back and chestnut-red streaks blended into its throat and chest feathers. His wings are dark olive edged in yellow, and he has a yellow eye ring. The female's plumage is yellow on the underside and distinctly greenish above. The chest streaks are very pale or completely absent. You may get a chance to see a Yellow Warbler in flight as it stalks an insect snack, displaying a variety of aerial techniques to obtain it. This bird is known for its ability to hover in midflight and even to hang from tree branches to grab its prey. Although it prefers spiders or insects, it will feed on any available berries during the winter months, when insect pickings are slim. The Yellow Warbler's song is a high-pitched, cheerful melody.

Male Yellow Warbler (adult)

Female Yellow Warbler with chicks

FOWL FACTS & FIGURES

LENGTH RANGE: 4.5–5 inches

WEIGHT: 0.3–0.4 ounce

WINGSPAN: 6–8 inches

SONG OR CALL: Song is a rapid, repetitive series of high, sweet notes. Call is a high-pitched *chirp*.

NEST: Cup-shaped, deep, lined inside and out with fur and fiber, normally found between V-shaped branches in a shrub or tree

EGGS:

Color: Gray, green, or white, with dark markings near heavy end

Incubation: 10–13 days

Clutch Size: 1–7 eggs

WHERE ARE THEY?

LEGEND
- Year Round
- Summer (breeding)
- Winter (nonbreeding)
- Migration

BEST TREES AND PLANTS FOR YOUR GARDEN

❶ Alder (genus *Alnus*) ❷ Wax myrtle (*Myrica cerifera*) ❸ White fir (*Abies concolor*): Alder, a flowering plant in the birch family, is widely known for its ability to attract moths, which can be a significant source of nutrition for the Yellow Warbler. The warbler also enjoys fruit, such as that of the wax myrtle. The waxy coating of this shrub's dusky blue berries led early North American colonists to dub the fruit "candleberry" because they often used the coating to make fragrant candles. If there is a stand of white fir on your property, you're in luck. Yellow Warblers favor those trees as cover from the weather and predators, and as nesting sites.

HOW TO ATTRACT YELLOW WARBLERS

Littleleaf Sumac

- Add a fountain or a water feature to your garden. The Yellow Warbler likes the sound of running water.
- Hang a suet feeder in your garden.
- Cultivate berry-producing plants, such as the littleleaf sumac (*Rhus microphylla*).

FAVORITE FOODS

Insects

Berries

Black-and-white Warbler

Mniotilta varia

ORDER: Passeriformes | FAMILY: Parulidae

The zebralike streaks of the male Black-and-white Warbler's plumage make it an easy bird to spot. The female looks very similar but is a duller black with more white distributed on the throat and neck. This little wood warbler has an unusually long hind toe and claw on each foot, a design that allows it to walk across branches and creep up and down tree trunks, where it forages for insects living in and on the bark. It feeds on a diet of caterpillars, spiders, and other tree-dwelling bugs. The Black-and-white Warbler is well known as an aggressive bird, and it will fight off or even attack another bird without much incentive. Its call is a high-pitched screeching sound.

Male Black-and-white Warbler (adult)

Female Black-and-white Warbler

FOWL FACTS & FIGURES

LENGTH RANGE: 4.3–5 inches

WEIGHT: 0.3–0.5 ounce

WINGSPAN: 7–9 inches

SONG OR CALL: Sings a distinct series of very high, short notes that sounds like a squeaky wheel.

NEST: Cup-shaped, made from dry leaves and other vegetation, normally found on the ground next to a tree

EGGS:

Color: Primarily white with brown and purple spots

Incubation: 10–12 days

Clutch Size: 4–6 eggs

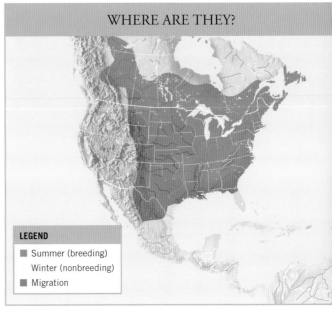

WHERE ARE THEY?

LEGEND

■ Summer (breeding)

Winter (nonbreeding)

▦ Migration

BEST TREES AND PLANTS FOR YOUR GARDEN

**❶ Dogwood (genus *Cornus*) ❷ Norway spruce (*Picea abies*)
❸ Grape (genus *Vitis*) ❹ Elaeagnus (genus *Elaeagnus*):**

If you have mature trees, such as dogwoods and Norway spruce, on your property, they will provide the Black-and-white Warbler with ideal places to forage or find shelter. Grapevines help to attract a steady, healthy supply of insects for this feisty little bird to enjoy. Elaeagnus is another insect- and spider-attracting shrub, which has very fragrant flowers and speckled fruit.

HOW TO ATTRACT BLACK-AND-WHITE WARBLERS

- Install a birdbath or a fountain in your garden.
- Place bits of fruit on a plate, and hang an oriole feeder that dispenses sugar water. The Black-and-white Warbler has been known to take sweet treats.
- Encourage trees and shrubs that have dense vegetation. They provide good places for roosting and foraging and offer protection from predators.

FAVORITE FOODS

Insects

Spiders

American Redstart

Setophaga ruticilla

ORDER: Passeriformes | FAMILY: Parulid

This small bird seems to be constantly busy, whether foraging, nest building, or protecting its territory. It moves about in a characteristically jittery fashion, almost as if it were dancing. The male's bold breeding plumage makes the American Redstart easily recognizable. His head and upperparts are coal black, and the wings and tail are streaked with bright orange. The female is predominately gray, and her upperparts and wings have subtle yellow streaks. Both sexes have a white underside. As his courtsh display, the male lowers his head and then raises and spreads his tail feathers. This display is not exclusive to th mating ritual, however, and he will sometimes perform it as a hunting tactic to scare prey out of hiding. Insects and other small invertebrates constitute the bulk of its diet, but the American Redstart adds some variety in the late summer by including berries and seeds on its menu.

Male American Redstart (adult)

Female American Redstart

FOWL FACTS & FIGURES

LENGTH RANGE: 4.3–5 inches

WEIGHT: 0.2–0.3 ounce

WINGSPAN: 6.3–7.5 inches

SONG OR CALL: Song is an alternating pair of very high notes.

NEST: Cup-shaped, tightly woven, bound together with spider webbing, usually found in the branches of trees

EGGS:

Color: Cream or white color, with dark marks

Incubation: 12 days

Clutch Size: 1–5 eggs

WHERE ARE THEY?

LEGEND
- Summer (breeding)
- Winter (nonbreeding)
- Migration

BEST TREES AND PLANTS FOR YOUR GARDEN

❶ Sugar maple (*Acer saccharum*) ❷ Shrimp plant (*Justicia brandegeana*) ❸ Elder (genus *Sambucus*) ❹ Nannyberry (*Viburnum lentago*) : The sugar maple is a natural habitat for a wide variety of insects, making it a feeding wonderland for the American Redstart. The shrimp plant is a popular shrub prized for its beautiful and unusual flowers, which resemble cooked shrimp. It will provide year-round interest in your garden and attract insects for the American Redstart to eat. Both elder and nannyberry can be grown as small trees or large shrubs. Birds love these trees because they produce edible berries and attract several species of insects, as well as provide exceptional roosting conditions.

HOW TO ATTRACT AMERICAN REDSTARTS

- Plant berry-bearing plants that attract insects.
- Hang a suet feeder in your garden or a tubular feeder filled with black-oil sunflower seeds.

FAVORITE FOODS

Spiders

Insects

Berries

Cedar Waxwing

Bombycilla cedrorum

ORDER: Passeriformes | FAMILY: Bombycillida

The plumage of the attention-grabbing Cedar Waxwing has a distinctive silky texture and smooth gradation of color ranging from red-brown on its upper body to pale yellow on its underside. The Cedar Waxwing's wings have red, waxlike tips on the secondary feathers—hence its name—and the tail feathers are yellow tipped. The exact color of the tips on the tail varies, depending on the bird's diet. Both sexes have tufted heads and black masks lined with white, but the male exhibits a darker chin patch than the female. In spring, the Cedar Waxwing gets its nourishment from sap, buds, and flowers, but come summer it switches to a largely fruit-based diet gleaned from fruit-bearing trees or berry bushes. It will feast on a huge variety of fruit through the winter. During breeding season, when it needs protein-rich foods, it will suppleme this diet with insects. Although sometimes considered a berry glutton, the Cedar Waxwing helps control the insec population in a garden.

Cedar Waxwing (adult)

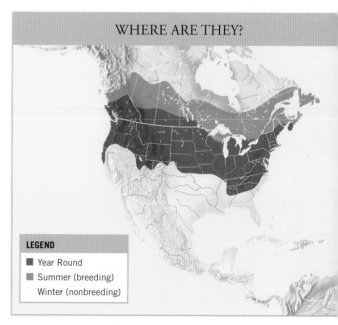

Members of a flock of Cedar Waxwings

FOWL FACTS & FIGURES

LENGTH RANGE: 5.5–7 inches

WEIGHT: 1–1.5 ounces

WINGSPAN: 8.7–11.8 inches

SONG OR CALL: Known for a variety of calls, including a slurred whistle and a high-pitched, flutelike tone.

NEST: Cup-shaped, bulky, often with intricate and time-consuming weaving, usually found between forked tree branches

EGGS:

Color: Light blue or gray, sometimes with black or gray spots

Incubation: 11–13 days

Clutch Size: 2–6 eggs

WHERE ARE THEY?

LEGEND

■ Year Round
■ Summer (breeding)
□ Winter (nonbreeding)

BEST TREES AND PLANTS FOR YOUR GARDEN

❶ Serviceberry (genus *Amalanchier*) ❷ Crabapple (genus *Malus*) ❸ Hawthorn (*Crataegus monogyna*) ❹ Eastern redcedar (*Juniperus virginiana*): Serviceberry is a great landscaping choice, with its delicate spring blooms and vibrant fall foliage. It also produces berries that the Cedar Waxwing will devour. This bird also feasts on the tart fruit of the crabapple. This tree's blossoms, which range from snowy white to deep pink, create a riot of springtime color. Crabapple needs a lot of space, so if you have a small plot, try a hawthorn tree instead. This tree produces cold-weather fruit and provides nesting sites and cover from predators. Of course, you can't go wrong with the Eastern redcedar. The Cedar Waxwing even gets its name from this berry-producing evergreen.

HOW TO ATTRACT CEDAR WAXWINGS

- Plant rich, fruit-bearing vegetation.
- Put out a tray bird feeder filled with raisins, apples, or currants.
- Install a birdbath, small pond, or fountain in your yard.

FAVORITE FOODS

Berries   Fruit   Flowers   Insects

Blue Jay

Cyanocitta cristata

ORDER: Passeriformes | FAMILY: Corvid

Despite its aggressive personality, the Blue Jay is prized for its beauty and is a welcomed guest in most backyards. This highly adaptable bird has a pronounced crest on its head and black markings framing a white face. Its back, wings, and tail are bright blue accented with black tips. Light refraction, not pigmentation, is responsible for this bird's blue plumage; if the feathers are crushed, the blue will disappear. Other than a slight size difference, with the male often larger, the sexes look alike. The Blue Jay's strong bill comes in handy for cracking open nuts and acorns and for eating tough grains, such as corn. It is skilled mimic able to replicate the call of hawks. The Blue Jay will eat spiders and occasionally raid the nests of other birds, where it will prey on eggs and nestlings.

Blue Jay (adult)

Fledgling Blue Jay

FOWL FACTS & FIGURES

LENGTH RANGE: 9.5–12 inches

WEIGHT: 2.5–3.5 ounces

WINGSPAN: 13–17 inches

SONG OR CALL: Song is a series of jumbled, woody notes. Call is a loud, aggressive squawk.

NEST: Cup-shaped, often lined with mud and roots, found in the high, outer branches of trees

EGGS:

Color: Light blue or brown with brown spots

Incubation: 17–18 days

Clutch Size: 2–7 eggs

WHERE ARE THEY?

LEGEND
- Year Round
- Summer (breeding)

BEST TREES AND PLANTS FOR YOUR GARDEN

❶ Eastern hemlock (*Tsuga canadensis*) ❷ White oak (*Quercus alba*) ❸ Many-flowered cotoneaster (*Cotoneaster multiflorus*) ❹ Wild cherry (*Prunus avium*): If your property is home to a stand of eastern hemlocks, many birds, including the Blue Jay, may already be nesting there. An oak tree in the backyard is also guaranteed to attract this bird. Among that oak's jay-attracting properties are its plentiful acorns. The many-flowered cotoneaster, a large shrub, provides this bird with both fruit and shelter. Although the abundant springtime blooms have a slightly unpleasant smell, the fall appearance of the fruit will attract the Blue Jay. The fruit of the wild cherry tree will also keep it returning to your garden.

HOW TO ATTRACT BLUE JAYS

- Fill a tubular feeder with sunflower seeds.
- Put out a tray feeder with an offering of cherries, chestnuts, and raw peanuts.
- Put out a small dish of crushed eggshells; the Blue Jay enjoys this calcium-rich treat.

FAVORITE FOODS

Seeds   Fruit   Acorns   Insects

Steller's Jay

Cyanocitta stelleri

ORDER: Passeriformes | FAMILY: Corvida

This stunning bird can be found west of the Rocky Mountains in North America. Like its close relative the Blue Jay, the Steller's Jay has primarily blue plumage, with no visible differences existing between the sexes. Its tail and underside are cornflower blue with subtle black markings, and its head, crest, and shoulders are dark, smoky blue or sometimes charcoal gray or black. Small streaks of white and light blue can also be seen on its head. The Steller's Jay is a lover of conifer seeds, nuts, and berries, but it is also quite a scavenger, and it will eat just about anything. It has an array of loud calls, which at tim resemble the grating call of a crow.

Steller's Jay (adult)

Fledgling Steller's Jay

FOWL FACTS & FIGURES

LENGTH RANGE: 11.5–13.5 inches

WEIGHT: 3.5–5 ounces

WINGSPAN: 17 inches

SONG OR CALL: Song is a throaty, random series of tweets. Calls are harsh, varied, and repetitive.

NEST: Cup-shaped, large, bulky, pasted together with mud. Often found in the branches of a conifer tree.

EGGS:

Color: Blue or green, with dark spots

Incubation: 16 days

Clutch Size: 2–6 eggs

WHERE ARE THEY?

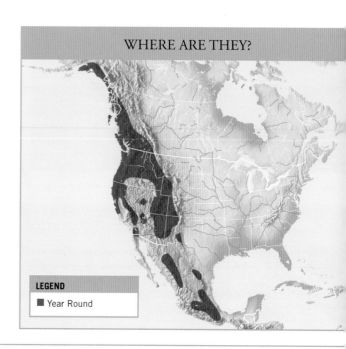

LEGEND

■ Year Round

BEST TREES AND PLANTS FOR YOUR GARDEN

❶ Pinemat manzanita (*Arctostaphylos nevadensis*) ❷ Fir (genus *Abies*) ❸ Akebono cherry plum (*Prunus* x *yedoensis*): To attract the Steller's Jay to your garden, plant pinemat manzanita. Ranging from a ground cover to a low-growing shrub, this plant bears a fruit that the jay eats. Steller's Jays are common in evergreen forests; if your property is near parkland or a forest, you may see this blue and black bird regularly. Firs are among its favorite trees. Akebono is an ornamental cherry plum tree that is widely available in garden nurseries. It is a popular choice among gardeners because it blooms early in spring. Its tiny, fragrant blossoms eventually give way to dark plum fruit, which continue well into the winter.

HOW TO ATTRACT STELLER'S JAYS

- Plant berry or fruit–bearing vegetation.
- Put out a tray feeder with an offering of black-oil sunflower, milo, and corn seeds, along with a selection of fruit and nuts. This jay particularly likes peanuts.

FAVORITE FOODS

| Seeds | Fruit | Nuts | Insects |

Barn Swallow

Hirundo rustica

ORDER: Passeriformes | FAMILY: Hirundinid

One of the most prolific and easily recognized of all of the swallows, the Barn Swallow has a shimmering, dark blue back, wings, head, and tail. The bird's distinctive shape includes curved wings and a deeply forked tail with long outer streamers. The length of these streamers is important to the female: the longer the tail of the male, the more favorable he will appear as a suitable breeding partner. Males with redder chests also tend to attract mor mates. The Barn Swallow catches its food while airborne, generally while flying low to the ground. This species has grown more widespread in tandem with the proliferation of humans because the bird often nests in man-made structures, such as inside barn eaves and under bridges. The Barn Swallow's song is a light and twittering warble.

Male Barn Swallow (adult)

Juvenile Barn Swallow

FOWL FACTS & FIGURES

LENGTH RANGE: 6–7.5 inches

WEIGHT: 0.6–0.7 ounce

WINGSPAN: 12.6–13.6 inches

SONG OR CALL: Song is a bubbling series of squeaks and gurgles.

NEST: Cup-shaped, lined with feathers and hair, often found attached to walls, underneath building eaves and ledges

EGGS:

Color: Cream or white, with dark specks

Incubation: 13-17 days

Clutch Size: 4–5 eggs

WHERE ARE THEY?

LEGEND

■ Year Round
■ Summer (breeding)
  Winter (nonbreeding)
▥ Migration

BEST TREES AND PLANTS FOR YOUR GARDEN

❶ Elm (*Ulmus americana*) ❷ Weigela (genus *Weigela*)
❸ Blackberry (genus *Rubus*) ❹ Black-eyed Susan
(*Rudbeckia hirta*): Attracting flying insects is key to luring the
Barn Swallow to a backyard or garden. A large tree such as the
American elm provides a spot for the swallow to perch and to survey
the surrounding area for food. The nectar-filled flowers of plants
such as weigela and blackberry bushes will certainly attract a variety
of flying insects. Black-eyed Susan is a bright yellow, midsummer-
blooming annual that is a beacon to a wide variety of winged insects.

HOW TO ATTRACT BARN SWALLOWS

- Install a birdbath, fountain, or pond in your backyard.
- If you have a barn or shed, make sure there is an opening,
  and place a nest cup or ledge in a high spot.
- Set out crushed eggshells in a jar lid feeder. These will
  supply the Barn Swallow with calcium at egg-laying time.

FAVORITE FOODS

Insects

Purple Martin

Progne subis

ORDER: Passeriformes | FAMILY: Hirundinida

The Purple Martin is the largest swallow in North America, and it is one of the most skillfully acrobatic in flight. Its call is a fluid warble, which matches its graceful flight pattern. The male is a shimmering blue-black; the female has a mixture of black and blue on her upper half with a paler, drab gray underside. Until maturity, the male closely resembles the female, which can make identification difficult. It takes the male two years to reach maturity and reveal his full breeding plumage. This bird feeds mainly while in flight; it rarely forages on the ground. In fact, it even skims the surface of water from the air to take a drink. The female typically lays her eggs in birdhouses or roosting nests. In parts of North America, the Purple Martin relies exclusively on humans for nesting sites.

Male Purple Martin (adult)

Female Purple Martin

FOWL FACTS & FIGURES

LENGTH RANGE: 7.5–8 inches

WEIGHT: 1.5–2 ounces

WINGSPAN: 15–16 inches

SONG OR CALL: Song is a series of sweet *purr* sounds. Call is a *clack* or *crack*.

NEST: Nest is of basic construction, composed of grass, mud, and twigs, found in the cavities and recesses of trees and buildings, as well as specially designed birdhouses

EGGS:

Color: White

Incubation: 15–18 days

Clutch Size: 1–8 eggs

WHERE ARE THEY?

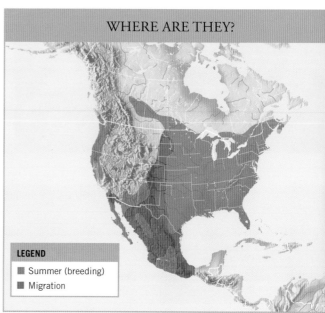

LEGEND
- Summer (breeding)
- Migration

BEST TREES AND PLANTS FOR YOUR GARDEN

❶ Chrysanthemum (genus *Chrysanthemum*) ❷ Common foxglove (*Digitalis purpurea*) ❸ Red buckeye (*Aesculus pavia*) ❹ Honeysuckle (genus *Lonicera*) ❺ Carpet bugle (*Ajuga reptans*): To bring the Purple Martin to your backyard and garden, focus on plants that are native to your area, because native insects won't feed on exotic plants. Perennials such as the chrysanthemum and common foxglove will keep your garden alive right through the fall. Both bloom in a variety of vibrant hues guaranteed to attract flying insects for the Purple Martin to eat. Deciduous red buckeye can be grown as a shrub or small tree. In summer, red buckeye bears drooping crimson panicles that also attract a multitude of insects. A decorative vine of honeysuckle combined with a flowering ground cover, such as carpet bugle, is another surefire way to provide this bird with a healthy supply of insects.

HOW TO ATTRACT PURPLE MARTINS

- Select an uncluttered area in your yard, and install a Purple Martin house.
- Install a birdbath or fountain, and consider reserving an area in your backyard for a pond.

FAVORITE FOODS

Berries

Spiders

Insects

Tree Swallow

Tachycineta bicolor

ORDER: Passeriformes | FAMILY: Hirundinida

The male Tree Swallow's back is a lustrous teal-blue that fades to black at the tips of its wings and tail. Its underside is pure white. It has a tiny beak, and its wings are only slightly larger than its body. The female has a brown upper half, but she still retains a hint of that shimmering blue. The Tree Swallow has been observed laying two broods in one mating season. When not mating, it will amass in gigantic flocks that can number in the thousands. At sunset, these flocks form massive swirling black clouds in the sky before the birds break up into small groups.

Male Tree Swallow (adult)

Female (left) and male Tree Swallows

FOWL FACTS & FIGURES

LENGTH RANGE: 4.5–6 inches

WEIGHT: 0.6–0.9 ounce

WINGSPAN: 11.8–13.8 inches

SONG OR CALL: Song is a repetitive, gurgling whistle.

NEST: Cup-shaped, made from grass and conifer needles, lined with feathers, placed in tree cavities

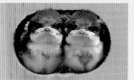

EGGS:

Color: White

Incubation: 13–16 days

Clutch Size: 2–8 eggs

WHERE ARE THEY?

LEGEND

- Year Round
- Summer (breeding)
- Winter (nonbreeding)
- Migration

BEST TREES AND PLANTS FOR YOUR GARDEN

❶ Wax myrtle (*Myrica cerifera*) ❷ Northern bayberry (*Myrica pensylvanica*) ❸ Dill (*Anethum graveolens*) ❹ Red-osier dogwood (*Cornus sericea*): Wax myrtle produces small wax-coated fruits that are a staple of the Tree Swallow's diet. Another member of the genus *Myrica*, the semievergreen bayberry shrub, also produces waxy berries that are highly prized by the Tree Swallow. Dill is a self-sowing, edible herb that resembles blades of green grass. Dogwoods, such as the red-osier, will add color to your yard or garden with their blossoms; the Tree Swallow feeds on the tree's fruit.

HOW TO ATTRACT TREE SWALLOWS

- If you have no empty tree cavities in your yard, erect a birdhouse. Tree swallows and bluebirds will often nest near each other.
- Plant ground cover grasses and flowers that attract insects.

FAVORITE FOODS

Berries　　　**Seeds**　　　**Insects**

White-breasted Nuthatch

Sitta carolinensis

ORDER: Passeriformes | FAMILY: Sittida

This small, sturdy songbird can often be seen hopping along tree trunks, sometimes upside down, sometimes sideways, foraging for insects. The male has a black crown, a white face and underside, and a gray-blue back. The female is gray all over. The bird's upturned bill is nearly as long as its head is wide. It uses its sharp bill to pry seeds from nuts and acorns, which it wedges into tree bark.

You may hear the White-breasted Nuthatch before you se it; its loud song has been described as a nasal *yank-yank*. Hardwood forests across North America are the usual habitat of this bird, and they particularly like nut trees and conifers, too. This monogamous bird mates for life. The male cares for new hatchlings for the first few days, but both parents share the duties afterward.

White-breasted Nuthatch, navigating headfirst

Male White-breasted Nuthatch (adult)

FOWL FACTS & FIGURES

LENGTH RANGE: 5–6 inches

WEIGHT: 0.6–1 ounce

WINGSPAN: 8–11 inches

SONG OR CALL: Song is a rapid, nasal whistle and a low-pitched *wha-wha-wha*.

NEST: Cup-shaped nest of feathers, fine grass, and bark strips, built in tree cavity or old woodpecker hole that has been lined with bark, fur, and lumps of soil

EGGS:

Color: Cream or pinkish white with brown, gray, or purple speckles or spots

Incubation: 13–14 days

Clutch size: 5–9 eggs

WHERE ARE THEY?

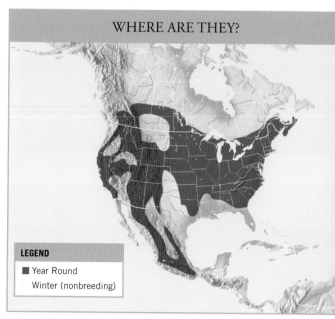

LEGEND

■ Year Round

　Winter (nonbreeding)

BEST TREES AND PLANTS FOR YOUR GARDEN

❶ Hickory (genus *Carya*) ❷ Paper birch (*Betula papyrifera*) ❸ Arborvitae (genus *Thuja*) ❹ Sunflower (*Helianthus annuus*): The White-breasted Nuthatch prefers mature conifers and nut trees as its habitat, so you'll have the best luck seeing them if you already have a stand of large trees such as hickory on or near your property. Woodland species such as paper birch also make eye-catching landscaping trees. Provide safe cover for this bird as it visits feeders by planting dense evergreen shrubs, such as arborvitae. The ever-popular sunflower produces gorgeous golden flowers through late summer before going to seed. Sunflower seeds will attract scores of birds, including the White-breasted Nuthatch.

HOW TO ATTRACT WHITE-BREASTED NUTHATCHES

- Fill feeders with sunflower seeds, unsalted peanuts, and suet.
- Erect a nuthatch-size birdhouse about 15 feet off the ground.
- Supply plenty of fresh water.

FAVORITE FOODS

Seeds

Nuts

Insects

Red-breasted Nuthatch

Sitta canadensis

ORDER: Passeriformes | FAMILY: Sittid

Its distinctive cinnamon-colored underside and smoky blue-gray back and wings make the Red-Breasted Nuthatch an easy bird to identify. It has a short tail and a straight, dark gray bill. The lower portion of its face is white with a black line accentuating the eyes and crown. The male and female look nearly identical, with the female showing a paler underside. A known food hoarder, the Red-breasted Nuthatch will stash food supplies in preparation for the lean winter months. It will not migrat in the winter if its environment provides enough sustainir resources. Climbing up, down, and sideways, it forages on tree trunks to glean insects and spiders. Its diet also includes conifer seeds. This nuthatch marks the entrance its nest with tree resin as a way to ward off intruders.

Male Red-breasted Nuthatch (adult)

Female Red-breasted Nuthatch

FOWL FACTS & FIGURES

LENGTH RANGE: 4–4.5 inches

WEIGHT: 0.3–0.5 ounce

WINGSPAN: 7–8 inches

SONG OR CALL: Song is a series of harsh, hornlike tones. Call is a short, repeated *tui-tui-tui.*

NEST: Bed of grass, strips of bark, and pine needles lined with fur, feathers, shredded bark, and fine grasses, usually found in dead trees, with resin applied to entrance

EGGS:

Color: White with a cream or pink tinge, with brown or red specks

Incubation: 12–13 days

Clutch Size: 2–8 eggs

WHERE ARE THEY?

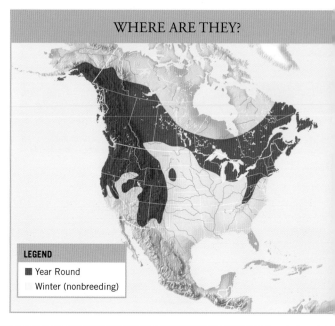

LEGEND

■ Year Round

□ Winter (nonbreeding)

BEST TREES AND PLANTS FOR YOUR GARDEN

❶ Red pine (*Pinus resinosa*) ❷ White spruce (*Picea glauca*) ❸ American beech (*Fagus grandifolia*) ❹ Fragrant thimbleberry (*Rubus odoratus*): The Red-breasted Nuthatch prefers conifer seeds, and every few years the red pine, which can reach 80 feet in height, produces a hardy seed supply. Another evergreen that it will flock to is the white spruce. This bird, as its name implies, also loves nuts, and the American beech produces tasty ones. The fragrant thimbleberry shrub has pink to purple flowers that turn into tiny berries. Both flower and berry attract insects, offering the nuthatch opportunities to forage for a protein-filled treat.

HOW TO ATTRACT RED-BREASTED NUTHATCHES

- Hang a suet ball made with chopped nuts, seeds, and fruit.
- Make a feeder out of conifer cones by spreading peanut butter on the cones, and then sprinkling the outside with seeds. Hang the homemade feeder from a branch or pole with a string.

FAVORITE FOODS

Conifer Seeds

Insects

Nuts

111

Brown Creeper

Certhia americana

ORDER: Passeriformes | FAMILY: Certhid[

If you can spot one, the Brown Creeper can be identified by its unique plumage pattern. Its underside is white, but its back is brown with white spots and streaks, so that this little bird virtually disappears as it inches up the side of a tree trunk. The only visible difference between the sexes is that the male has a slightly larger bill. The Brown Creeper forages by spiraling its way up the trunk of a tree, meticulously gleaning every insect it finds until it reaches the top. It then parachutes down to the base of another tree and begins its feeding ritual again. The Brown Creepe[is often found in mixed-species flocks that may include chickadees, nuthatches, kinglets, and woodpeckers.

Brown Creeper (adult)

Brown Creeper

FOWL FACTS & FIGURES

LENGTH RANGE: 4.5–5.5 inches

WEIGHT: 0.2–0.4 ounce

WINGSPAN: 7–8 inches

SONG OR CALL: Song is a series of high-pitched twitters. Call is a high, singular note.

NEST: Cup-shaped, built upon a base of discarded cocoons and spider egg cases, usually hidden in the recesses of loose or broken tree bark

EGGS:

Color: White, often with brown, pink, or red marks

Incubation: 13–17 days

Clutch Size: 1–8 eggs

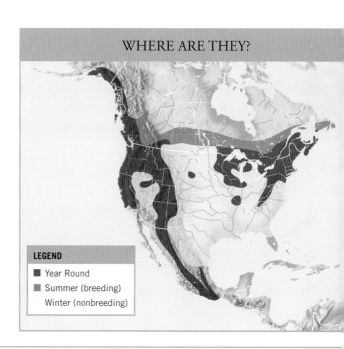

WHERE ARE THEY?

LEGEND
- Year Round
- Summer (breeding)
- Winter (nonbreeding)

BEST TREES AND PLANTS FOR YOUR GARDEN

**❶ Shagbark hickory (*Carya ovata*) ❷ Pine (genus *Pinus*)
❸ White oak (*Quercus alba*) ❹ Balsam fir (*Abies balsamea*):**
Rough-barked trees are essential to creepers because they hold numerous insects. The shagbark hickory, with its shaggy layers of bark, makes a great hunting ground for the Brown Creeper. This bird will wind its way up many species of pine. Another choice is the white oak. Its creviced bark is home to scores of insects. The textured bark of balsam fir is a Brown Creeper favorite. This fir offers foraging, good nesting conditions, and an adequate seed supply.

HOW TO ATTRACT BROWN CREEPERS

- Plant one or more trees; select a variety with bark that is attractive to larvae.
- Provide a fresh source of water by installing a birdbath or other water feature in your garden.

FAVORITE FOODS

Spiders

Seeds

Insects

Black-capped Chickadee

Poecile atricapillus

ORDER: Passeriformes | FAMILY: Parid[

This mild-mannered bird gets its name from its striking black cap and bib. The Black-capped Chickadee is a petite bird, and its tail is relatively long in proportion to its body. Its wings are dark with white edging. The Black-capped Chickadee has a complex system of calls with more than 13 different vocal sounds, but it sings a very simple song. It will often hang upside down from a perch to hun tree-dwelling insects and larvae, which make up a signifi-cant portion of its diet. It will, however, occasionally eat seeds and berries. The Black-capped Chickadee is an agile bird but a slow flyer. It generally travels in flocks, with an established hierarchy among group members.

Black-capped Chickadee (adult)

Black-capped Chickadee, gripping a tree trunk

FOWL FACTS & FIGURES

LENGTH RANGE: 4.5–6 inches

WEIGHT: 0.3–0.5 ounce

WINGSPAN: 6.3–8.3 inches

SONG OR CALL: Song differs depending on geographical location, but normally consists of a pair of slow, melodic notes. Call is clipped and high-pitched.

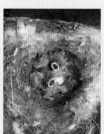

NEST: Composed of moss and fur, usually hidden inside an excavated tree cavity

EGGS:

Color: White with small brown or red specks

Incubation: 12–13 days

Clutch Size: 1–13 eggs

WHERE ARE THEY?

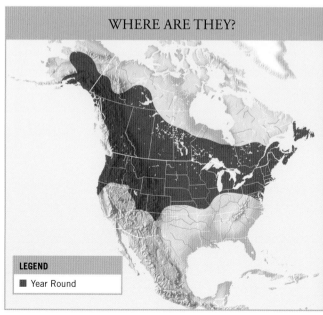

LEGEND

■ Year Round

BEST TREES AND PLANTS FOR YOUR GARDEN

❶ American sweetgum (*Liquidambar styraciflua*) ❷ Willow (genus *Salix*) ❸ Cockspur hawthorn (*Crataegus crus-galli*) ❹ Checkerberry (*Gaultheria procumbens*) ❺ Huckleberry (*Gaylussacia baccata*): Existing trees in your backyard are great for attracting this small, friendly bird. The American sweetgum is a medium to large tree that provides plenty of elbow room for the Black-capped Chickadee to perch and forage. The graceful willow tree also offers a suitable place for this bird to forage. Many species of willow trees and shrubs grow in the colder, moister areas of the Northern Hemisphere, where the chickadee lives. The cockspur hawthorn is a small tree or shrub that bears edible berries in late summer though midwinter. Checkerberry is a creeping shrub that provides excellent ground cover. It produces small red berries from the fall to the spring. A huckleberry shrub will provide dark purple or blue berries for consumption toward the end of the summer.

HOW TO ATTRACT BLACK-CAPPED CHICKADEES

- Hold out a handful of birdseed as you stand very still. The Black-capped Chickadee is often willing to eat right from a palm.
- Hang a suet feeder or a tubular feeder filled with black-oil sunflower seeds and peanuts.
- Plant dense ground cover for foraging.

FAVORITE FOODS

Berries   Seeds   Insects

Tufted Titmouse

Baeolophus bicolor

ORDER: Passeriformes | FAMILY: Parida

This small songbird is a frequent visitor to parks, gardens, and backyard bird feeders. It can be identified by its gray plumage and tufted crown and the black square above its bill. The Tufted Titmouse forages for food on the ground or in trees, and it is often observed hanging upside down on a branch as it hunts insects. It especially enjoys eating caterpillars, and its diet also includes seeds, berries, and nuts, which the bird stockpiles. The Tufted Titmouse is a friendly and curious bird, perching on windowsills an other places in close proximity to humans. This bird lives year-round in the Northeast, where it may be found flocking with other birds, such as the Black-capped Chickadee

Tufted Titmouse (adult)

Tufted Titmouse (right) with a Black-capped Chickadee

FOWL FACTS & FIGURES

LENGTH RANGE: 5.5–6.5 inches

WEIGHT: 0.6–1 ounce

WINGSPAN: 7.9–10.2 inches

SONG OR CALL: Song is a shrill, insistent whistle. Call is a harsh, nasal *caw*.

NEST: Bed constructed from damp, soft vegetation, often lined with a variety of animal hair, and found in natural or preexisting cavities

EGGS:

Color: Cream or white, with dark spots

Incubation: 12–14 days

Clutch Size: 3–9 eggs

WHERE ARE THEY?

LEGEND

■ Year Round

BEST TREES AND PLANTS FOR YOUR GARDEN

❶ Elder (genus *Sambucus*) ❷ American beech (*Fagus grandifolia*) ❸ Oak (genus *Quercus*) ❹ Joe-pye weed (*Eupatorium maculatum*): You can't go wrong by planting an elder shrub. The Tufted Titmouse, along with many other species, eagerly gobbles up these dark blue-purple fruits. If there are American beech or oak trees on your property, count yourself lucky. The American beech, with its silver-gray bark and deep green leaves, prefers shade to sun and produces edible nuts that attract the Tufted Titmouse. Oaks attract an array of insects, and their fruit, the acorn, is a valuable source of nutrition for the Tufted Titmouse and other birds. The oak is known for its longevity and visual appeal, as well as the host of insect and bird life each tree can support. To add color to your garden, plant tall stalks of joe-pye weed. In summer, its clouds of rose-purple flowers will draw butterflies. In winter, it will supply food and cover for the Tufted Titmouse.

HOW TO ATTRACT TUFTED TITMICE

- Place a nesting box or a birdhouse approximately 10 feet above the ground.
- Hang a suet bird feeder in your yard, or put out a hopper or tray bird feeder filled with black-oil sunflower seeds and peanuts. Fruit and peanut butter are also nice winter treats.

FAVORITE FOODS

Berries   Seeds   Insects

Golden-crowned Kinglet

Regulus satrapa

ORDER: Passeriformes | FAMILY: Regulid

Known for being not easily frightened by humans, the Golden-crowned Kinglet is a very tiny, very active bird that constantly flicks its wings. As its name suggests, a bright crown of yellow-gold sits atop its head, which is edged in jet black with an outer band of snowy white. Its underside is white, and its upperparts, chest, and face are gray. The plumage on its back also has a bit of yellow blended into the gray, and the wings have two white bars. The sexes look nearly identical, but the male has orange blended into his crown, which can be hard to spot. The Golden-crowned Kinglet prefers coniferous woods, where it gleans insects and their eggs from the bark of trees.

Male Golden-crowned Kinglet (adult)

Female Golden-crowned Kinglet

FOWL FACTS & FIGURES

LENGTH RANGE: 3–4.5 inches

WEIGHT: 0.1–0.3 ounce

WINGSPAN: 5.5–7 inches

SONG OR CALL: Song is a series of thin notes followed by gurgling. Call is a trio of very high-pitched *tsee* tones.

NEST: Cup-shaped, deep, often lined with fur and lichen, usually found hanging from twigs or tree branches

EGGS:

Color: Dull white with brown spots

Incubation: 14–15 days

Clutch Size: 3–11 eggs

WHERE ARE THEY?

LEGEND

- Year Round
- Summer (breeding)
- Winter (nonbreeding)
- Migration

BEST TREES AND PLANTS FOR YOUR GARDEN

❶ Douglas fir (*Pseudotsuga menziesii*) ❷ White spruce (*Picea glauca*) ❸ Sugar bush (*Rhus ovata*) ❹ Rhododendron (genus *Rhododendron*): Evergreen trees, such as Douglas fir and white spruce, will give the Golden-crowned Kinglet all it needs to thrive. Sugar bush can be grown as a shrub or as a small tree; its spring flowers bloom in pink or white, and the small, hairy, wax-covered fruit it bears will help to attract many insects for this bird to eat. The landscaper's staple rhododendron is a thicket-forming shrub that does best in moist soil and makes for excellent foraging. Its showy flowers add life to suburban lawns across North America.

HOW TO ATTRACT GOLDEN-CROWNED KINGLETS

Speckled Alder

- Plant trees and dense shrubs that provide the Golden-crowned Kinglet with good foraging territory, such as speckled alder (*Alnus incana*).
- Install a birdbath in your garden.
- Introduce flowering shrubs.

FAVORITE FOODS

Spiders   **Insect Eggs**   **Insects**

Bushtit

Psaltriparus minimus

ORDER: Passeriformes | FAMILY: Aegithalid

Only one member of the Aegithalidae, or long-tailed tit family, lives in North America: the tiny but stocky Bushtit. Its large head and seemingly nonexistent neck give it its chubby appearance. The plumage of both the male and the female is plain brown-gray, although a variation called the Black-eared Bushtit will show black ear patches. The male bird has dark eyes; the female's eyes are yellow. The Bushtit prefers scrubby woodland in its western North America habitat, where it forages for insects and spiders, but it is also quite at home in suburban parks, gardens, an backyards. The industrious Bushtit is known for crafting elaborate hanging nests that feature hooded openings. Th busy little bird even plays mother's helper, assisting with the feeding of other Bushtits' chicks. Extremely social and gregarious, it often integrates with flocks of other bird spe cies, such as chickadees and wood warblers.

Male Bushtit (adult)

Female (at top) with other Bushtits

FOWL FACTS & FIGURES

LENGTH RANGE: 2.8–4 inches

WEIGHT: 0.1–0.2 ounce

WINGSPAN: 7 inches

SONG OR CALL: Song is a constant, vibrating twitter. Call is a short yelp or a high-pitched shriek.

NEST: Large, gourd-shaped, elaborately constructed with a covered entrance, and usually lined with feathers, fur, and other soft materials; found hanging from the branches of a tree

EGGS:

Color: White

Incubation: 12–13 days

Clutch Size: 4–10 eggs

WHERE ARE THEY?

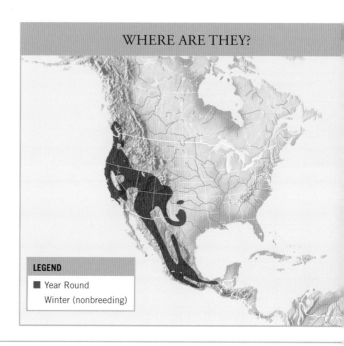

LEGEND

■ Year Round

Winter (nonbreeding)

BEST TREES AND PLANTS FOR YOUR GARDEN

❶ California juniper (*Juniperus californica*) ❷ Fir (genus *Abies*) ❸ Blackberry (genus *Rubus*): The California juniper is an ornamental shrub that provides an excellent foraging area and protective cover. It bears clusters of waxy blue berries that attract insects. A member of the fir group would be a perfect tree for the Bushtit, one that gives it a place to forage for insects and find shelter from the elements, while offering sturdy branches to hang a nest. Both the fruit and the flowers of the blackberry attract insects, and the Bushtit can use its brambly branches for shelter.

HOW TO ATTRACT BUSHTITS

- Install a birdbath or other water feature in your garden, because Bushtits will often congregate around a water source.
- Introduce trees, herbs, and shrubs that simulate a brushy or woodland habitat.
- Hang a suet feeder to supply wintertime nourishment.

FAVORITE FOODS

Spiders   Insects

American Robin

Turdus migratorius

ORDER: Passeriformes | FAMILY: Turdida

Who hasn't seen this busy bird hopping across a lawn or grassy park only to stop, standing alert with head cocked and beak tilted upward as it surveys the area? The American Robin is part of the thrush family and is the most widespread of its kind in North America. It returns from its winter migration very early in the season, so first sightings of this common garden bird at the close of winter are a popular sign that spring is on its way. The male American Robin has a reddish brown chest, a dark head with small white eye crescents, and a gray tail and wings. The female is very similar but with less contrast. It forage mainly on the ground, searching for small fruits and earth worms, which it pulls out of the ground with its beak. Th bird is fairly shy, and it tends to stick with its flock.

American Robin (adult)

Juvenile American Robin

FOWL FACTS & FIGURES

LENGTH RANGE: 8–11 inches

WEIGHT: 2.7–3 ounces

WINGSPAN: 12–16 inches

SONG OR CALL: Song is a lengthy series of moderately paced, reedy notes. Call is a passive gurgle and a more pronounced warning *yeep*.

NEST: Cup-shaped, constructed primarily of grass and twigs; lined and stiffened with mud, and usually located on covered tree branches, but occasionally found under eaves or in gutters or other structures

EGGS:

Color: Bright blue or green

Incubation: 12–14 days

Clutch Size: 3–5 eggs

WHERE ARE THEY?

LEGEND

■ Year Round

■ Summer (breeding)

Winter (nonbreeding)

BEST TREES AND PLANTS FOR YOUR GARDEN

❶ Common hackberry (*Celtis occidentalis*) ❷ Apple (*Malus domestica*) ❸ Japanese maple (*Acer palmatum*) ❹ Pine (genus *Pinus*): The American Robin is known for its love of worms, but it also eagerly devours a variety of fruits and berries. The common hackberry provides summer-ripening fruit that will last into winter. Plant one of the hundreds of varieties of orchard apples, and both you and the birds can enjoy its fall harvest. The robin will also nest in a mature apple tree. A maple tree, such as the spectacular Japanese maple, will also provide the American Robin with a place to roost and forage for insects, as will many species of pine.

HOW TO ATTRACT AMERICAN ROBINS

- Mount a nesting shelf on the side of your house.
- Don't use lawn chemicals. The American Robin searches in the grass for its favorite treat: worms.
- Mulch your flower beds with fall leaves to provide prime foraging areas.

FAVORITE FOODS

Berries   Fruit   Insects

Eastern Bluebird

Sialia sialis

ORDER: Passeriformes | FAMILY: Turdida

The Eastern Bluebird is a common garden bird belonging to the thrush family. You can find this delightful species almost anywhere in North America east of the Rocky Mountains. The head and upper body of the male are a vibrant blue; its throat and breast are a reddish brown; and its underside is white. The female is similar to the male but with blue tones shimmering through her gray head and upper body. The Eastern Bluebird is a veritable connoisseur of insects, but it also enjoys sweet fruits when its main food source is scarce. You can often see it on roadsides, sitting on a tree branch or a fence post waiting for a delicious morsel to fly or crawl past.

Eastern Bluebird (adult)

Female Eastern Bluebird

FOWL FACTS & FIGURES

LENGTH RANGE: 6.3–8.3 inches

WEIGHT: 1–1.5 ounces

WINGSPAN: 9.8–13 inches

SONG OR CALL: Song is a concise warbling. Call is similar, but lower pitched.

NEST: Cup-shaped, woven with grass and conifer needles, situated in a cavity or nest box

EGGS:

Color: Light blue, sometimes white

Incubation: 11–19 days

Clutch Size: 2–7 days

WHERE ARE THEY?

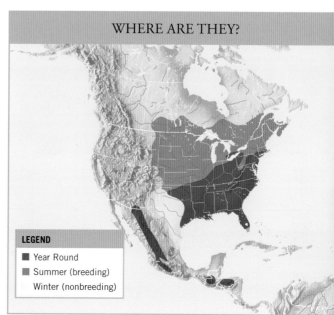

LEGEND
- Year Round
- Summer (breeding)
- Winter (nonbreeding)

BEST TREES AND PLANTS FOR YOUR GARDEN

❶ Blueberry (genus *Vaccinium*) ❷ Black chokeberry (*Aronia melanocarpa*) ❸ Fly honeysuckle (*Lonicera xylosteum*) ❹ Clove currant (*Ribes aureum*): There is sure to be a variety of blueberry appropriate for your area that will lure the Eastern Bluebird. Some produce fruit in summer, others as late as fall. The black chokeberry, an Eastern Bluebird favorite, makes a great shrub or small tree. Its fruit ripens late in the spring. Fly honeysuckle is a dwarf species that grows as a radiating mound. It produces fragrant flowers that attract many flying insects; its tiny red fruit also attracts many six-legged treats. Add an easy-to-grow clove currant shrub to your garden. Its fruit is a bluebird pleaser. In spring, the clove currant's golden yellow flowers fill the air with a clovelike scent before giving way to amber-yellow berries.

HOW TO ATTRACT EASTERN BLUEBIRDS

- Find an open area to erect a bluebird house; face the opening east.
- Plant a mix of fruit- and berry-bearing shrubs.
- Add some apple slices and other fruit segments to a tray feeder.

FAVORITE FOODS

Spiders

Berries

Insects

Hermit Thrush

Catharus guttatus

ORDER: Passeriformes | FAMILY: Turdidae

Is it any wonder that poets such as Walt Whitman and T. S. Eliot have included this plain brown bird in their poetry? A clear, bright whistle introduces the melodious song of the Hermit Thrush—a song so lovely that it more than makes up for the bird's unremarkable appearance. It is a medium-size bird with a brown back, a ruddy tail, and a pale underside with dark brown to black speckles on its chest. Its eyes are framed by a thin white eye ring. The male and female look alike. The Hermit Thrush prefers a moist forest or woodland habitat and spends the entire year in North America. It winters in the southern portions before heading north to breed, typically nesting in ravines and other sheltered sites. During the warmer seasons, the Hermit Thrush hops about the ground with tail cocked and wings flicking, foraging for insects. In colder weather, it supplements its diet with berries, buds, and fruit.

Hermit Thrush (adult)

Hermit Thrush

FOWL FACTS & FIGURES

LENGTH RANGE: 6–7 inches

WEIGHT: 0.5–1 ounce

WINGSPAN: 9.25–11 inches

SONG OR CALL: Song is a clear whistle followed by a melodic, flutelike warble. Call is a low *chuck* or harsh *screy*.

NEST: Cup-shaped, woven from grass, feathers, and wool, lined with fine material, such as grasses, hair, moss, bark, and willow catkins; found on the ends of tree branches or on the ground

EGGS:
Color: Light blue with dark spots
Incubation: 12–14 days
Clutch Size: 3–7 eggs

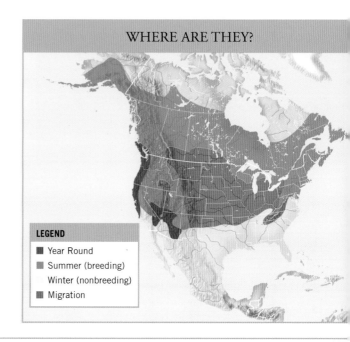

WHERE ARE THEY?

LEGEND

■ Year Round
■ Summer (breeding)
  Winter (nonbreeding)
■ Migration

BEST TREES AND PLANTS FOR YOUR GARDEN

❶ Black willow (*Salix nigra*) ❷ Western serviceberry (*Amelanchier alnifolia*) ❸ Lemonade sumac (*Rhus integrifolia*) ❹ California holly (*Heteromeles arbutifolia*):
The wispy leaves of the black willow lend this small shrubby tree a delicate air. Its downy catkins will supply a Hermit Thrush with soft material to line its nest. The purple-blue berries of the serviceberry tree are avian crowd pleasers, and the Western serviceberry will particularly appeal to the Hermit Thrush. This thrush will also take advantage of the lemonade sumac. Grown as a shrub or small tree, this sumac offers foraging turf along with edible berries. As its name suggests, you can use its berries to make a lemonade-flavored summer drink. The California holly not only supplies bright red berries for the Hermit Thrush to eat, it drops leaf litter, through which this bird will eagerly forage in its search for insects.

HOW TO ATTRACT HERMIT THRUSHES

- Allow fall leaves to pile up a bit; the Hermit Thrush likes to forage for insects by digging through leaf litter.
- Add a variety of fruits including oranges, raisins, and apple slices to your tray bird feeder.

FAVORITE FOODS

Berries **Buds** **Fruit** **Insects**

Eastern Phoebe

Sayornis phoebe

ORDER: Passeriformes | FAMILY: Tyrannida

The Eastern Phoebe, one of the most common birds in North America, is a small member of the diverse tyrant flycatcher family. It is gray or olive in color with a light gray breast. The Eastern Phoebe's head and tail are a slightly darker shade than its back, and its underside varies in hue from white to yellow. The adult male and female look alike. This bird is well adapted to living alongside humans, and it will often nest in urban areas and backyards. A solitary bird, the Eastern Phoebe rarely travels with a flock. It prefers to hunt solo from a low perch, scanning the area for bugs and flying insects before setting off for a chase. It also supplements its diet with berries. Occasionally, the Eastern Phoebe wags its tail. The song of this bird is a rough whistle that is reminiscent of its name: *fee-bee.*

**Eastern Phoebe
(adult)**

Eastern Phoebe with catch

FOWL FACTS & FIGURES

LENGTH RANGE: 5.5–6.7 inches

WEIGHT: 0.6–0.7 ounce

WINGSPAN: 10.2–11 inches

SONG OR CALL: Song is a simple, bubbly series of two notes. Call is a simple *cheep.*

NEST: Cup-shaped; usually affixed with mud to an eve, wall, or other structure

EGGS:

Color: White, sometimes with dark markings
Incubation: 16 days
Clutch Size: 2–6 eggs

WHERE ARE THEY?

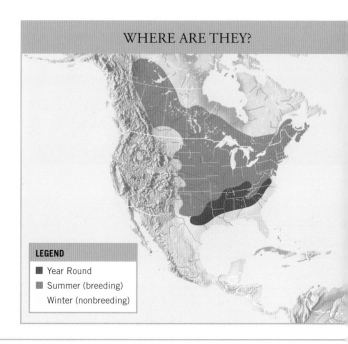

LEGEND

■ Year Round
■ Summer (breeding)
　Winter (nonbreeding)

BEST TREES AND PLANTS FOR YOUR GARDEN

❶ Spicebush (*Lindera benzoin*) ❷ Fennel (*Foeniculum vulgare*) ❸ Marigold (*Tagetes erecta*) ❹ Sumac (genus *Rhus*): The easiest way to lure a flycatcher such as the Eastern Phoebe is to plant insect-attracting vegetation. The berry-producing spicebush is a deciduous shrub with clusters of yellow flowers. Its main attraction for the Eastern Phoebe is not the berry fruit but the prevalence of insects found within the spicebush's leaves. Herbs, such as fennel, and annual flowers, such as marigold, also attract plenty of bugs. To attract insects and supply the Eastern Phoebe with seeds, add a few rows of cheery marigolds to your garden. A sumac shrub will help to attract insects for the Eastern Phoebe while gracing your garden with rich fall foliage. It also provides seeds and berries that this bird will eat when insects are scarce.

HOW TO ATTRACT EASTERN PHOEBES

- Mount a nesting shelf approximately 8 to 12 feet above the ground.
- Create brush piles during the fall and winter so that insects have a place to nest.
- Plant berry-bearing vegetation to attract insects.

FAVORITE FOODS

Spiders

Insects

Berries

Great Crested Flycatcher

Myiarchus crinitus

ORDER: Passeriformes | FAMILY: Tyrannidae

The Great Crested Flycatcher is a large bird in the tyrant flycatcher family. Both the male and the female sport a brown- or olive-colored back, reddish brown wings and tail, and a gray throat and breast. The belly and the underside of the tail are a bold lemon yellow. It breeds in mixed forests and woodlands across eastern North America. Unlike other flycatchers, the Great Crested will nest inside trees. It uses natural cavities or those abandoned by woodpeckers, lining the cavity with snakeskin or other crinkly material such as onion skins or plastic wrappers. You can often spot this treetop dweller high in the trees, flitting from branch to branch. The Great Crested Flycatcher also forages while flying, hunting for small insects and invertebrates, or eating small fruits.

Great Crested Flycatcher (adult)

Great Crested Flycatcher

FOWL FACTS & FIGURES

LENGTH RANGE: 6.7–8.3 inches

WEIGHT: 1–1.5 ounces

WINGSPAN: 12.75–14 inches

SONG OR CALL: Call is a mournful, whistling *wee-eep* or a forceful, grating *buzz*.

NEST: Cup-shaped, made of leaves, hair, trash, and even snakeskin; sometimes built inside a cavity on top of a base of trash

EGGS:
Color: Light pink or white, with specks and streaks all over
Incubation: 13–15 days
Clutch Size: 4–8 eggs

WHERE ARE THEY?

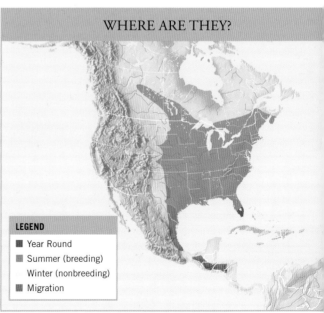

LEGEND
■ Year Round
■ Summer (breeding)
　Winter (nonbreeding)
▦ Migration

BEST TREES AND PLANTS FOR YOUR GARDEN

❶ Cosmos (*Cosmos bipinnatus*) ❷ Pin cherry (*Prunus pensylvanica*) ❸ American sycamore (*Platanus occidentalis*) : Food, shelter, and a place to nest—that's all the Great Crested Flycatcher needs. To supply food, plant insect-attracting flowers, such as cosmos. To supply "dessert," plant a pin cherry. This small tree, grown mostly in northern parts of the United States and in southern Canada, is sometimes referred to as the "bird cherry" because it produces small red fruit that is a delectable treat for many birds. Small cavities in trees such as the American sycamore provide the Great Crested Flycatcher with a place to shelter and build a nest.

HOW TO ATTRACT GREAT CRESTED FLYCATCHERS

- If possible, leave dead trees on your property; they provide valuable nesting sites. Alternatively, hang a birdhouse approximately 10 feet above the ground.
- Introduce fruit and berry-bearing vegetation.

FAVORITE FOODS

Insects　　　　**Berries**　　　　**Fruit**

Western Kingbird

Tyrannus verticalis

ORDER: Passeriformes | FAMILY: Tyrannida

This tyrant flycatcher has a gray chest and head. Its belly is yellow; its tail is black, squared-tipped, and edged with white. Like other flycatchers, the Western Kingbird scouts out insects and then darts from its perch to catch its prey. The Western Kingbird is well adapted to living in close proximity to humans, and it will readily nest in man-made structures, such as barns and bridges. Its highly aggressive nature helps to ensure the safety of its nest from predators such as hawks. This kingbird spends the breeding season in western North America; it migrates to South America for the winter. On occasion, however, a late-migrating bird can be spotted on the East Coast in fall.

Western Kingbird (adult)

Western Kingbird feeding chicks

FOWL FACTS & FIGURES

LENGTH RANGE: 8–9.5 inches

WEIGHT: 1.3–1.6 ounces

WINGSPAN: 15–16 inches

SONG OR CALL: Song is a busy, jumbled series of gurgling notes. Call is a similar but briefer note.

NEST: Cup-shaped, open, lined with a variety of soft material such as cotton and hair; normally found in trees or on tall, slender structures such as poles and posts

EGGS:
Color: Cream or white, with dark markings on the heavy end
Incubation: 18–19 days
Clutch Size: 2–7 eggs

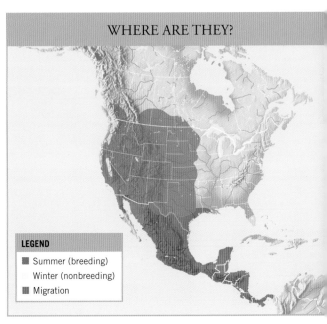

WHERE ARE THEY?

LEGEND
■ Summer (breeding)
□ Winter (nonbreeding)
■ Migration

BEST TREES AND PLANTS FOR YOUR GARDEN

**❶ Crabapple (genus *Malus*) ❷ Lantana (genus *Lantana*)
❸ Coriander (*Coriandrum sativum*) ❹ Jacob's ladder
Polemonium caeruleum):** The only difficulty in choosing a crabapple is deciding which of the 36 or more varieties you like best. This flowering deciduous plant is available as a tree and as a shrub; both bear edible berries or fruit. The lantana, a creeping evergreen native to the West Coast, produces nutritious berries that the Western Kingbird enjoys. It's hardy and tolerates low temperatures well. Planting a patch of insect-attracting herbs, such as coriander, will also lure this bird to your garden. Jacob's ladder is a flowering fern, the leaves of which grow in a pattern resembling a ladder.

HOW TO ATTRACT WESTERN KINGBIRDS

Common Evening Primrose

- Plant flowers that attract flying insects, such as the cheery yellow common evening primrose (*Oenothera biennis*).
- Create an open, uncluttered area in your garden. The Western Kingbird is attracted to lawns and clearings. This bird also enjoys perching on the limbs of high trees, fences, and utility wires.

FAVORITE FOODS

Insects

Berries

133

Red-eyed Vireo

Vireo olivaceus

ORDER: Passeriformes | FAMILY: Vireonid

This common but elusive bird has a distinctive call, which takes the form of a repetitive question-and-answer tone. The Red-eyed Vireo spends many hours a day singing the same song, and you can often detect it by sound rather than sight. Its wings and back are olive green and its underside is white. Its eyes are red, accented with a black eye line and white eyebrow, and its crown is gray. The male and female look very similar, with the male bei just slightly larger. This woodland bird is at home in urba and suburban areas with tree-filled parks and backyards. enjoys a heavily insect-laden diet and uses its hooked bill glean caterpillars and aphids from tree foliage.

Red-eyed Vireo
(adult)

Red-eyed Vireo

FOWL FACTS & FIGURES

LENGTH RANGE: 4.5–5 inches

WEIGHT: 0.4–0.9 ounce

WINGSPAN: 9.1–9.8 inches

SONG OR CALL: Song is slurred with a pronounced end note that is either high- or low-pitched.

NEST: Deep cup-shaped, often crafted from needles, lichen, and spider webbing; found between the forks of tree branches

EGGS:
Color: Gray or white, with brown or red specks
Incubation: 11–14 days
Clutch Size: 3–4 eggs

WHERE ARE THEY?

LEGEND
■ Summer (breeding)
  Winter (nonbreeding)
■ Migration

BEST TREES AND PLANTS FOR YOUR GARDEN

❶ Wild cherry (*Prunus avium*) ❷ Grape (genus *Vitis*) ❸ Black tupelo (*Nyssa sylvatica*) ❹ Staghorn sumac (*Rhus typhina*):
The flowering wild cherry will blossom in the spring and enliven your garden or yard with its vibrant flowers. The Red-eyed Vireo will appreciate this deciduous tree for its small fruit, which also ripens in the spring. A summer grapevine will be a popular spot for this and many other birds, thanks to its fruit-bearing and insect-attracting qualities. In the autumn, the larger black tupelo will take center stage as it displays its fall foliage and its fruit fully ripens. In winter, the Red-eyed Vireo will eat the fruit of the staghorn sumac.

HOW TO ATTRACT RED-EYED VIREOS

Saucer Magnolia

- Plant plenty of berry-bearing and insect-attracting vegetation in your yard.
- Introduce trees such as dogwood (genus *Cornus*) or saucer magnolia (*Magnolia* x *soulangeana*), which will harbor abundant leaf-dwelling insects.

FAVORITE FOODS

Insects

Berries

Downy Woodpecker

Picoides pubescens

ORDER: Piciformes | FAMILY: Picidæ

The Downy is the smallest woodpecker in North America and is found in almost every area of the continent. Its upper half is black with a white stripe running down the middle, and its underside is white. The head is black and white, and the wings are black with white spotting. The male is distinguished from the female by a small red mark on his crown. In winter, the Downy Woodpecker will often roost in the cavity of a tree. Its comparatively diminutive size is an advantage, enabling it to feed where larger woodpeckers cannot. It lives primarily on a diet of insects, spiders, fruits, and seeds, but during the cold winter months, it will readily supplement its diet with offerings from humans, such as suet from a backyard bird feeder.

Male Downy Woodpecker (adult)

Female Downy Woodpecker

FOWL FACTS & FIGURES

LENGTH RANGE: 5.5–6.7 inches

WEIGHT: 0.7–1 ounce

WINGSPAN: 9.8–12 inches

SONG OR CALL: Call is a musical *nay* or *winny*, not unlike a high-pitched horse. Also widely known for its drumming, an insistent striking against tree bark that is audible over a wide area, used to establish its territory and during mating.

NEST: Simple nest hole located in an excavated cavity and lined with wood chips

EGGS:

Color: White

Incubation: 12 days

Clutch Size: 3–8 eggs

WHERE ARE THEY?

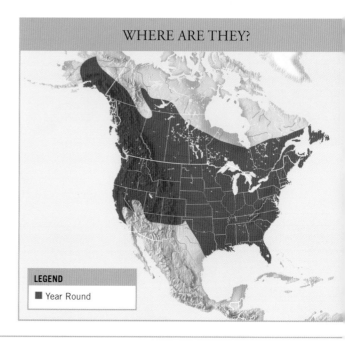

LEGEND

■ Year Round

BEST TREES AND PLANTS FOR YOUR GARDEN

❶ Oak (genus *Quercus*) ❷ Maple (genus *Acer*) ❸ Virginia creeper (*Parthenocissus quinquefolia*): The Downy Woodpecker has varied tastes, so finding a plant to tempt it is easy. It will eat fruit and nuts, such as acorns, so an oak is a welcome backyard addition. This little woodpecker will also slurp up the sap leaking from a maple where a larger woodpecker drilled a hole. Virginia creeper is a vine that produces small, hard berries that are poisonous to mammals but are an avian staple throughout winter.

HOW TO ATTRACT DOWNY WOODPECKERS

- Hang a tubular bird feeder filled with cracked corn and sunflower seeds.
- Set out bread scraps, doughnuts, and fruit on a tray feeder.
- Offer a suet feeder filled with beef suet mixed with nuts and seeds.

FAVORITE FOODS

Berries   **Acorns**   **Seeds**   **Insects**

Pileated Woodpecker

Dryocopus pileatus

ORDER: Piciformes | FAMILY: Picida

The Pileated Woodpecker is a large, beautiful but elusive North American woodpecker. It has black and white stripes on its head and throat, and it reveals white feathers when it spreads its wings to fly. The head of both male and female is capped with a brilliant red crest. The adult male has an extra red stripe extending from his gray bill to his throat. The Pileated Woodpecker's call is a ringing tone that sounds like cackling—and inspired the Woody Woodpecker cartoon character. Its wood-pecking drum is loud and repetitive, often audible over great distances. It pecks distinctive rectangular holes into trees as it forages for food, and it will nest inside the cavities of dead trees. I diet consists primarily of insects, such as beetle larvae and carpenter ants, but it also likes berries, fruit, and nuts.

Male Pileated Woodpecker (adult)

A Pileated Woodpecker feeding its young

FOWL FACTS & FIGURES

LENGTH RANGE: 15.5–19 inches

WEIGHT: 8.8–12.3 ounces

WINGSPAN: 26–29.5 inches

SONG OR CALL: Call is a harsh, repeated *squawk* or *chuk*; also broadcasts a drumming sound by forcefully banging its beak against tree trunks.

NEST: Simple nest built inside the cavity of a dead tree, with lining of wood chips

EGGS:

Color: White

Incubation: 15–18 days

Clutch Size: 1–6 eggs

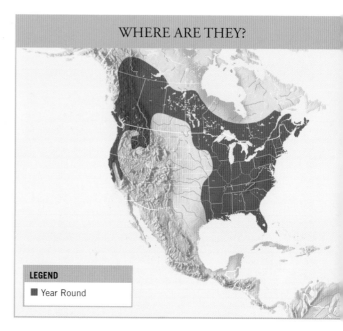

WHERE ARE THEY?

LEGEND

■ Year Round

BEST TREES AND PLANTS FOR YOUR GARDEN

❶ **Eastern arborvitae (*Thuja occidentalis*)** ❷ **Western hemlock (*Tsuga heterophylla*)** ❸ **Cherry (genus *Prunus*)**: The Pileated Woodpecker is a large bird and needs mature trees to make its nest, generally finding one at least 70 years old. If you are lucky enough to have an old tree, such as an eastern arborvitae or a western hemlock, you may find a pair nesting in a drilled-out cavity. The eastern arborvitae is often trained as a hedge shrub, but it will reach 65 feet if left alone. For quicker results, plant a fruit-bearing tree, such as cherry, which will supply this bird with a late summer treat.

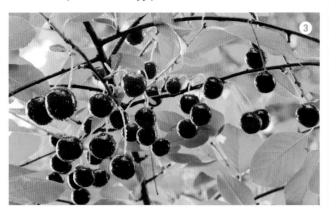

HOW TO ATTRACT PILEATED WOODPECKERS

- Leave dead or decaying wood, such as a fallen tree, that might be in your garden; this is rich with wood-dwelling insects that the woodpecker thrives on.
- Install a birdbath.

FAVORITE FOODS

Berries   **Nuts**   **Seeds**   **Insects**

Red-headed Woodpecker

Melanerpes erythrocephalus

ORDER: Piciformes | FAMILY: Picida

This elegant tricolored bird has a bold crimson red head; a black tail, wings, and upper half; and a white chest and underside. The male and female Red-headed Woodpecker are identical. The male will aggressively defend its territory from attack and may try to conquer other nests in the area. Its call is loud, harsh, and especially sharp when it is defending its turf. It is common for this bird to prey on insects, which it hunts with a long, hooked bill. It eats a wide range of other foods, such as seeds, sap, nuts, and fruit, and it is one of the few woodpeckers to hoard food. The Red-headed Woodpecker population has declined in direct correlation to the destruction of dead or rotten trees, which are essential nesting sites for this bird in its natural habitat.

Red-headed Woodpecker (adult)

Red-headed Woodpecker storing seeds

FOWL FACTS & FIGURES

LENGTH RANGE: 7.5–9 inches

WEIGHT: 2–3.5 ounces

WINGSPAN: 15–17 inches

SONG OR CALL: Call is an aggressive, crowing sound. Shares the habit of drumming with other members of the woodpecker family.

NEST: Simple nest inside cavities within dead tree trunks or branches

EGGS:

Color: White

Incubation: 12–14 days

Clutch Size: 4–7 eggs

WHERE ARE THEY?

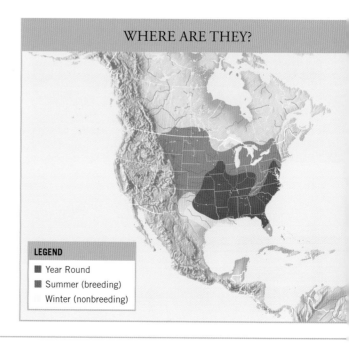

LEGEND

■ Year Round

■ Summer (breeding)

  Winter (nonbreeding)

BEST TREES AND PLANTS FOR YOUR GARDEN

❶ **American beech (***Fagus grandifolia***)** ❷ **Sugar maple (***Acer saccharum***)** ❸ **Northern red oak (***Quercus borealis***):** American beech, sugar maple, and northern red oak are all excellent tree choices that will help you attract a Red-headed Woodpecker to your yard. The beech will supply it with plenty of nuts and the oak with lots of acorns. A sugar maple provides great foraging for insects and a sweet sappy snack. All three provide ideal places for woodpeckers to nest—and they lend vivid fall color to the landscape.

HOW TO ATTRACT RED-HEADED WOODPECKERS

- Hang a tubular feeder fitted with a generous number of perches and filled with seeds, such as cracked corn.
- Leave a dead or rotting tree standing, as long as it is far from any houses.

FAVORITE FOODS

| Tree Sap | Nuts | Seeds | Insects |

Northern Flicker

Colaptes auratus

The Northern Flicker, a member of the woodpecker family, is one of the few birds in this group to migrate in the fall. Many of the flickers in the northernmost reaches of this species' range travel southward to spend winter's coldest months in sunnier climes. The adult of both sexes has a grayish brown back with black barring, a black crescent on the chest, and a prominent white rump. The male also has a small red swash near his beak. There are two separate forms of the Northern Flicker: the Yellow-shafted and the Red-shafted. The two variations differ only slightly in appearance, most notably in the respective yellow or red coloring of the feathers under the tail and wings. Ants are the favorite food of the Northern Flicker, but this bird also eats fruits, berries, nuts, and seeds. It is one of the only woodpeckers to forage on the ground in search of food. The call of the Northern Flicker is similar to that of its larger relative the Pileated Woodpecker, but the Flicker's call is not as harsh.

Male Red-shafted Northern Flicker (adult)

Male Yellow-shafted Northern Flicker

FOWL FACTS & FIGURES

LENGTH RANGE: 11–12.5 inches

WEIGHT: 4–5.5 ounces

WINGSPAN: 18–20 inches

SONG OR CALL: A variety of calls, including a hornlike squawking, as well as a more subtle *wik-wik-wik*. Like other woodpeckers, the Northern Flicker produces a mellow drumming sound.

NEST: Deep compartment with a narrow entrance, dug into dead or rotting wood, lined with wood chips

EGGS:

Color: White

Incubation: 11–13 days

Clutch Size: 5–8 eggs

WHERE ARE THEY?

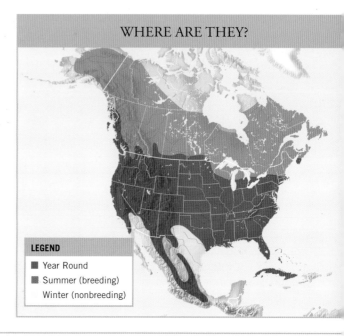

LEGEND
- Year Round
- Summer (breeding)
- Winter (nonbreeding)

BEST TREES AND PLANTS FOR YOUR GARDEN

❶ Whitebark pine (*Pinus albicaulis*) ❷ Creeping juniper (*Juniperus horizontalis*) ❸ Common hackberry (*Celtis occidentalis*) ❹ Coralbells (genus *Heuchera*): The Northern Flicker often nests in a large tree, such as a mature whitebark pine, but you can plant low-growing shrubs, such as the creeping juniper, to give it an ideal place to forage and a safe place to nest. The common hackberry tree has nutritious calcium-filled berries that the bird will happily consume. The perennial coralbells will give your garden stunning ground cover in addition to providing an excellent foraging site for the Northern Flicker and a variety of other birds. Its nectar-filled flowers attract an abundance of insects, which enhances its value as a bird-attracting plant.

HOW TO ATTRACT NORTHERN FLICKERS

- Hang up a birdseed feeder or a homemade pinecone peanut butter bird feeder.
- Avoid clearing away dead or rotting wood from your yard or property.
- Keep a birdbath filled with clean, fresh water.

FAVORITE FOODS

Berries   Fruit   Nuts   Seeds   Insects

Yellow-billed Cuckoo

Coccyzus americanus

ORDER: Cuculiformes | FAMILY: Cuculida

You are more likely to hear the loud, throaty song of the Yellow-billed Cuckoo than to catch a glimpse of this languid and elusive bird. In the South, it is often referred to as the storm or rain crow because it often calls on a hot, dry day just before a downpour or a thunderstorm. The Yellow-billed Cuckoo's upper half is brown, while its lower half and chin are white. The underside of its tail is black with white spots. The female is slightly larger than the male. It i a patient hunter, and it will lie in wait for some time befor moving in on its prey, which includes insects, caterpillars, cicadas, frogs, and small lizards. This is a migratory bird, which does most of its traveling by night on its journey from North to South America. The Yellow-billed Cuckoo will, on occasion, lay an egg or two in another species' nes

Yellow-billed Cuckoo (adult)

Yellow-billed Cuckoo

FOWL FACTS & FIGURES

LENGTH RANGE: 10.2–11.8 inches

WEIGHT: 2–2.5 ounces

WINGSPAN: 15–17 inches

SONG OR CALL: Call is a series of loud *caws* and *coos.*

NEST: Simple, shallow platform, consisting of bark and twigs; found in shrubs and trees

EGGS:

Color: Blue or green

Incubation: 9–11 days

Clutch Size: 1–5 eggs

WHERE ARE THEY?

LEGEND

- Summer (breeding)
- Winter (nonbreeding)
- Migration

BEST TREES AND PLANTS FOR YOUR GARDEN

❶ Wild prairie rose (*Rosa arkansana*) ❷ Virginia creeper (*Parthenocissus quinquefolia*) ❸ Inkberry (*Ilex glabra*) ❹ Weigela (genus *Weigela*) : To attract the Yellow-billed Cuckoo, plant shrubs and other vegetation that attract insects, provide cover, and produce berries. The dense cover of the wild prairie rose bush offers concealment from predators. Once the flowers fade, this shrub will yield nutritious rosehips. Virginia creeper produces nectar-filled flowers that attract bees and other insects. It is a prolific climber and prized for its vibrant fall color, growing best in partial sunlight. The short perennial inkberry bears small white blossoms and black berries. The berries appear in summer shortly after the plant flowers. Inkberry will continue to bear fruit until fall. The weigela, which comes in several different forms, including a climbing shrub, is a source of nutrients for insects that attract this cuckoo.

HOW TO ATTRACT YELLOW-BILLED CUCKOOS

- Plant berry-bearing vegetation, such as a raspberry bush (genus *Rubus*) or a grape vine (genus *Vitis*).
- Introduce leafy trees and dense shrubs that provide good roosting and foraging places.
- Install a fountain, pond, or other water feature in your yard.

FAVORITE FOODS

Berries   Amphibians   Seeds   Insects

Mourning Dove

Zenaida macroura

ORDER: Columbiformes | FAMILY: Columbidæ

Adaptable to a wide range of habitats, the Mourning Dove is ubiquitous in North America. Its sorrowful cooing song and the whistling sound made by its wings as it launches into flight make it easily recognizable. The Mourning Dove is a subtle sandy brown or pearl gray with a paler, pink-brown underside. It has short, rounded wings spotted with black, and its long gray tail feathers are edged with white. Beneath its eye is a unique black comma-shaped mark. The adult male and female look alike. This bird is accustomed to living in urban areas, and it will nest and breed in the open. It eats a mainly vegetarian diet of seeds, and it forages on the ground.

Mourning Dove (adult)

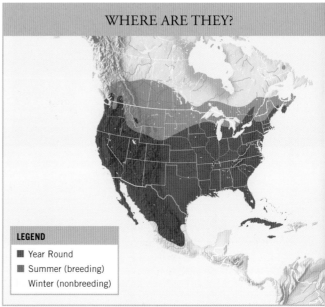

Mourning Dove with chicks

FOWL FACTS & FIGURES

LENGTH RANGE: 9–13.5 inches

WEIGHT: 3.5–6 ounces

WINGSPAN: 14–18 inches

SONG OR CALL: Song for males is a loud, somber *coo* when mating.

NEST: Unlined shallow cup, loosely assembled from grass, needles, and twigs; found in a variety of trees or on the ground

EGGS:

Color: White

Incubation: 14 days

Clutch Size: 2 eggs

WHERE ARE THEY?

LEGEND

■ Year Round
■ Summer (breeding)
Winter (nonbreeding)

BEST TREES AND PLANTS FOR YOUR GARDEN

❶ Cosmos (*Cosmos bipinnatus*) ❷ Pink bachelor's button (*Centaurea pulcherrima*) ❸ Sunflower (*Helianthus annuus*) ❹ Blue spruce (*Picea pungens*): It doesn't take much to lure the Mourning Dove to your garden—just plant plenty of high-yield seed producers. Classic garden flowers that produce small nigerlike seeds, such as cosmos and pink bachelor's button, add color and attract this bird. A grouping of sunflowers adds life to backyard, and the annual's big flower heads are a source of the seeds that few birds will turn down. An evergreen tree such as a blue spruce will not only supply seeds but also offer this bird a safe nesting site.

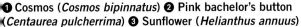

HOW TO ATTRACT MOURNING DOVES

- Put out a tray bird feeder with a large platform and plenty of room for perching. Fill the tray with seeds, such as cracked corn, millet, and, for a special treat, peanuts.
- You can recycle slightly stale bread by breaking it up and leaving it outside for the Mourning Dove.

FAVORITE FOODS

Seeds   **Nuts**

Anna's Hummingbird

Calypte anna

ORDER: Apodiformes | FAMILY: Trochilid

The Anna's Hummingbird is named after Anna Masséna, a nineteenth-century Italian duchess. The male has an iridescent red throat and head, a gray underside, and a bronzy iridescent green upper half. The female is mostly gray with traces of shimmering green.

This nectar-loving bird prefers flowering trees, and it will even suck sap straight from a tree trunk. During breeding season, the male goes to great lengths to impress the fema with elaborate diving displays. He is also fond of singing, rare trait among hummingbirds.

Anna's Hummingbird (adult)

Female Anna's Hummingbird

FOWL FACTS & FIGURES

LENGTH RANGE: 3.5–4 inches

WEIGHT: 0.1–0.2 ounce

WINGSPAN: 4.75–5 inches

SONG OR CALL: Call is a brittle, scratching pattern. Its beating wings also make a humming sound as this bird flies.

NEST: Cup-shaped and composed of plant fibers woven together with spider webbing; outside covered with soft vegetation

EGGS:

Color: White

Incubation: 14–19 days

Clutch Size: 2 eggs

WHERE ARE THEY?

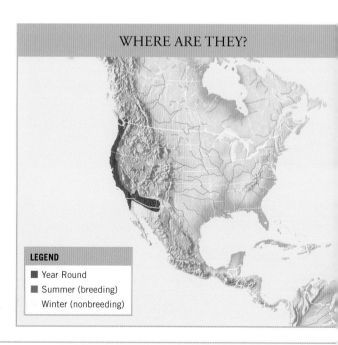

LEGEND

■ Year Round
■ Summer (breeding)
Winter (nonbreeding)

BEST TREES AND PLANTS FOR YOUR GARDEN

❶ Bougainvillea (genus *Bougainvillea*) **❷** Aloe vera (*Aloe vera*)
❸ Fireweed (*Epilobium angustifolium*) **❹** Mexican bush sage
(*Salvia leucantha*): Versatile bougainvillea is a woody flowering
evergreen that you can train to grow as a vine or bushy shrub. Its
bunches of nectar-filled, cup-shaped blooms come in shades of
magenta, purple, pink, red, orange, and gold. The succulent aloe vera
grows well in arid climates, where Anna's Hummingbirds are most
often found. In summer, tall shoots of bright yellow to red flowers
burst from the center of this plant's thick, spiky leaves. The Anna's
Hummingbird will find a stand of fireweed, with its spiky sprays of
pink-lavender flowers, as attractive as you will. This plant has long
been used to make candies, syrups, and jellies. Spikes of fuzzy violet,
trumpet-shaped flowers make Mexican bush sage a garden standout.
This hummingbird pleaser can reach about 4 feet tall.

HOW TO ATTRACT ANNA'S HUMMINGBIRDS

- Look for plants with trumpet- or cup-shaped flowers in
  hot colors, such as red, orange, deep pink, and purple.
- Hang a hummingbird feeder near a window.
- Introduce sap-producing trees, such as maple (genus
  Acer) or cherry (genus *Prunus*).

FAVORITE FOODS

Tree Sap

Nectar

Insects

Black-chinned Hummingbird

Archilochus alexandri

ORDER: Apodiformes | FAMILY: Trochilida

The Black-chinned Hummingbird has iridescent green wings and back, green flanks, and a white underbelly. The male has a black head and chin with a thin purple band around his throat, which is only visible at certain angles. The female has a pale throat. Like all nectar-sipping hummingbirds, this bird gathers its food by hovering close to the food source and using its long tongue to reach the nectar inside. This method of eating helps pollinate the flowers it visits. The Black-chinned Hummingbird will sometimes eat insects, but its diminutive size means that it is also prey to larger birds on the lookout for food. The male makes a distinct sound as he dives, a move he will perform as part of his mating ritual. The call of the Black-chinned Hummingbird is a high-pitched *tik*.

Black-chinned Hummingbird (adult)

Female Black-chinned Hummingbird

FOWL FACTS & FIGURES

LENGTH RANGE: 3–3.5 inches

WEIGHT: 0.1–0.2 ounce

WINGSPAN: 3.5–4.3 inches

SONG OR CALL: Call is a variety of *chirp* and *tik* sounds. It also emits a beelike humming sound, presumably produced by the rapid beat of its wings while in flight.

NEST: Cup-shaped and flexible; expands as the hatchlings grow

EGGS:

Color: White

Incubation: 12–16 days

Clutch Size: 2 eggs

WHERE ARE THEY?

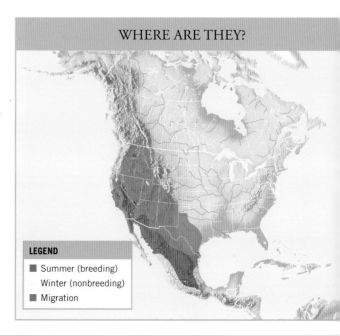

LEGEND
■ Summer (breeding)
Winter (nonbreeding)
▦ Migration

BEST TREES AND PLANTS FOR YOUR GARDEN

❶ Columbine (genus *Aquilegia*) ❷ Cape fuschia (*Phygelius capensis*) ❸ Purple coneflower (*Echinacea purpurea*) ❹ Rocky Mountain penstemon (*Penstemon strictus*): There are many species of columbine, a perennial plant with beautiful, unusual flowers that will attract the Black-chinned Hummingbird. The pendulous flowers of Cape fuschia are the perfect shape for a hummingbird's questing bill. These ornamental plants look lovely spilling over the sides of hanging planters and patio containers. Purple coneflower is a garden classic that attracts scores of birds, including the Black-chinned Hummingbird, which will drop by for a sip of its nectar. The showy blue flowers of the tall, graceful Rocky Mountain penstemon also attract this bird. This plant is known for its hardiness and ability to tolerate drought conditions.

HOW TO ATTRACT BLACK-CHINNED HUMMINGBIRDS

- Plant nectar-producing flowers such as butterfly bush (*Buddleia davidii*) or red sage (*Salvia officinalis*).
- Hang a hummingbird feeder.
- Introduce trees and shrubs with thick branches that offer safe roosting places.

FAVORITE FOODS

Tree Sap   Nectar   Insects

Ruby-throated Hummingbird

Archilochus colubris

ORDER: Apodiformes | FAMILY: Trochilid.

The tiny Ruby-throated Hummingbird, the only hummingbird of eastern North America, has a shimmering, metallic green upper body, black tail and wings, and grayish white underside. As its name suggests, the male flashes a ruby red patch on his throat. In certain lights, this ruby hue can appear black. The female is a little larger than the male, her plumage is more muted, and she has no throat marking. This minuscule bird has the ability to fly sideways, straight up and down, and backward, a sk it needs in removing its long beak from its food source aft it has finished feeding. This feisty bird prefers the edges of forests, open woods, meadows, and grasslands, and is a frequent visitor to gardens, parks, and backyards, where it will readily sip nectar from a hummingbird feeder.

Male Ruby-throated Hummingbird (adult)

Female Ruby-throated Hummingbird

FOWL FACTS & FIGURES

LENGTH RANGE: 3–3.5 inches

WEIGHT: 0.1–0.2 ounce

WINGSPAN: 3–4.5 inches

SONG OR CALL: Call is a series of high-pitched *chip* and *clik* sounds. It also makes a low-pitched humming sound as it flies.

NEST: Tiny and cup-shaped; constructed from flexible materials that are held together with spider webbing and tree sap

EGGS:

Color: White

Incubation: 12–14 days

Clutch Size: 1–3 eggs

WHERE ARE THEY?

LEGEND
- Summer (breeding)
- Winter (nonbreeding)
- Migration

BEST TREES AND PLANTS FOR YOUR GARDEN

❶ Bee balm (genus *Monarda*) ❷ Shrimp plant (*Justicia brandegeana*) ❸ Garden phlox (*Phlox paniculata*) ❹ Ivy geranium (*Pelargonium peltatum*): The rich red to purple blooms of the perennial bee balm are sure to attract the Ruby-throated Hummingbird to your garden. Bee balm's spiderlike flowers supply nectar and attract desirable insects. Hummingbirds won't resist stopping by a shrimp plant. This showy shrub bears flowers that come in colors from yellow to brick red. In the salmon-colored version the blooms closely resemble the plant's namesake. Like the Ruby-throated Hummingbird itself, garden phlox is native to eastern North America. The slender green stems of garden phlox, which can reach 3 feet high, hold up blooms ranging in color from snowy white to bubblegum pink to deep lavender. You can attract hummingbirds even if you have limited space. Plant a few nectar-rich ivy geraniums in window boxes or hanging planters.

HOW TO ATTRACT RUBY-THROATED HUMMINGBIRDS

- Hang a hummingbird feeder in your yard.
- Plant nectar-producing flowers.
- Introduce sap-producing trees, such as maple (genus *Acer*) or birch (genus *Betula*), into your garden.

FAVORITE FOODS

Tree Sap **Nectar** **Insects**

Garden Gallery

In this inspirational gallery, you will find bird-attracting gardens from many different climates and regions of the US and Canada and in many different styles and sizes. Get inspired to make minor or dramatic updates to your own home garden!

Trumpet honeysuckle, which is a great plant for attractin Baltimore Orioles needs something to grow up on, lik this rustic garden fence.

This Florida garden mixes tall tropical plants and low flowers.

omfortably seated in the shelter of a leafy canopy, you could spend a happy hour or more just admiring the nearby plants and siting feathered friends.

onds are great for attracting birds and other wildlife, but they are even more effective if you ensure water movement, as has een done with the fountain in this pond.

This Colorado mountain home needed a garden that would draw birds in both warm summers and freezing winters. The wildflowers are gorgeous when in bloom, and the flowerheads still provide tempting seeds after the first snowfall.

This spacious yard uses the sheds at the end of it as an anchor point for a vine-covered arbor where you can sit quietly and wait for the birds to join you.

erennials and dwarf evergreen shrubs edge this low deck with flowers and year-round greenery. A hanging basket might become surprise nesting spot for the right bird species.

his yard contains a great mix of flowering plants, leafy plants, tall trees, short bushes, and minimal open spaces—a perfect ombination to draw many kinds of birds.

These homeowners have chosen to place hummingbird feeders in small patch of organized floral variety, ensuring they get a good view of any drinkers. They can afford the lawn area and small, concentrated floral area because of all the old, tall trees around that will help attract birds.

...unded by large shrubs, this naturalistic stroll garden harbors birds, butterflies, and bees.

Brick pillars on either side of a path's entrance onto a terrace add distinction and highlight the path's position, creating a separation between the wild bird-friendly area and the neat relaxing area for humans.

Visually appealing to people and attractive to birds, the dogwood tree in front of this house will bring feathered visitors that are visible from the windows.

You can still draw birds if you live in the city. This Boston home has plenty of window planters to do the job. Don't forget to include planters on upper floors to keep birds away from roaming cats. The pre-existing trees on this street encourage birds to stay as well.

his design suits its landscape and climate with its mix of cacti, yuccas, and wildflowers found in southwestern gardens. Maybe bird will choose one of the cacti to build a nest.

Walls smothered in flowering climbers, such as roses, clematis, and honeysuckle, create color as well as informality. You'll love the smells, and the birds will love the plentiful perches and hiding places.

A riot of flowers and bushes draws visitors (both human and avian) into this yard. The birds have a little feeder poking up from amidst all the hiding places.

The focus of this gardener's efforts are the roses, but plentiful feeders and a shady, treed area provide food and shelter for birds.

ose mounds of foliage and a liberal sprinkling of flowers flank a gravel walk in this "cottage" garden. Walking on the noisy
avel might scare off visitors, so stick to the patio for birdwatching.

m for as many different plants as possible so that the ground is completely covered, providing privacy and shelter for creatures.

This backyard garden concentrates many different flower species into separate beds that are easy for the owners to walk through and enjoy.

is busy and varied landscape and all of its visitors can be admired while you're floating in the water.

your best to keep "barren" areas, such as lawns and paths, to a minimum. Replace them as much as possible with dense antings like this.

Coneflowers are common bird-attracting plants that mix in well with a lush and dense variety of other greenery.

This modern garden incorporates flowers, stones, green bushes, and a birthbath as separate "units."

is dramatic planting plays on the contrasts between foliage and flowers. Spiky agaves rise above the colorful flowers of low-wing verbena. The variety is great for attracting different species of birds with different personalities and needs.

Water gardens are an absolute haven for many types of wildlife, not just birds; you'll attract sparkling damselflies and fun amphibians, too.

Perfect birthbath placement: these birdbaths are away from trees and foliage, making birds comfortable because they can see predators approaching. The owner of this yard has chosen to focus flowers and feeders along the fence.

Hostas are great ground covers for shaded areas that birds will love.

all grasses, Russian sage, coneflowers, and avian accommodation create a beautiful setting for watching both birds and utterflies.

Naturally sculptured flat top rocks from northwest Oregon are placed in a beautifully landscaped backyard among a variety of erennial evergreens and shrubs.

Plant Hardiness Zone Maps

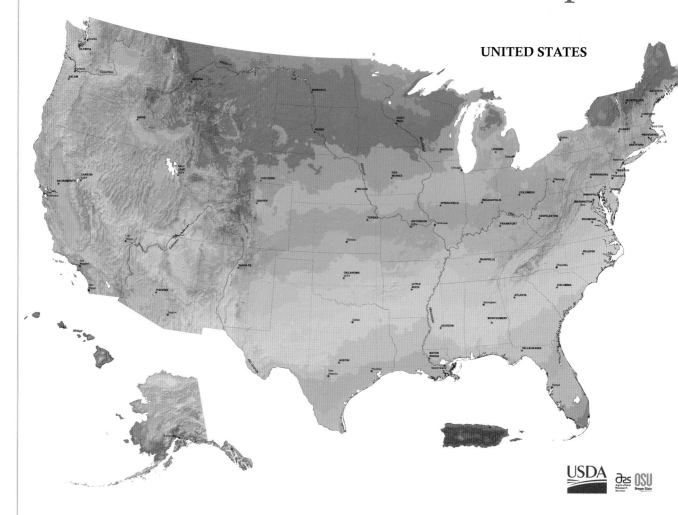

UNITED STATES

RANGE OF AVERAGE ANNUAL EXTREME MINIMUM TEMPERATURE

TEMP (°F)	ZONE	TEMP (°C)	TEMP (°F)	ZONE	TEMP (°C)	TEMP (°F)	ZONE	TEMP (°C)
-60 to -55	1a	-51.1 to -48.3	-15 to -10	5b	-26.1 to -23.3	30 to 35	10a	-1.1 to 1.7
-55 to -50	1b	-48.3 to -45.6	-10 to -5	6a	-23.3 to -20.6	35 to 40	10b	1.7 to 4.4
-50 to -45	2a	-45.6 to -42.8	-5 to 0	6b	-20.6 to -17.8	40 to 45	11a	4.4 to 7.2
-45 to -40	2b	-42.8 to -40	0 to 5	7a	-17.8 to -15	45 to 50	11b	7.2 to 10
-40 to -35	3a	-40 to -37.2	5 to 10	7b	-15 to -12.2	50 to 55	12a	10 to 12.8
-35 to -30	3b	-37.2 to -34.4	10 to 15	8a	-12.2 to -9.4	55 to 60	12b	12.8 to 15.6
-30 to -25	4a	-34.4 to -31.7	15 to 20	8b	-9.4 to -6.7	60 to 65	13a	15.6 to 18.3
-25 to -20	4b	-31.7 to -28.9	20 to 25	9a	-6.7 to -3.9	65 to 70	13b	18.3 to 21.1
-20 to -15	5a	-28.9 to -26.1	25 to 30	9b	-3.9 to -1.1			

From the United States Department of Agriculture (USDA)
website, *https://planthardiness.ars.usda.gov*

CANADA

RANGE OF AVERAGE ANNUAL EXTREME MINIMUM TEMPERATURE

TEMP (°F)	ZONE	TEMP (°C)	TEMP (°F)	ZONE	TEMP (°C)	TEMP (°F)	ZONE	TEMP (°C)
-70 to -60	0a/b	-56.7 to -51.1	-30 to -25	4a	-34.4 to -31.7	5 to 10	7b	-15.0 to -12.2
-60 to -55	1a	-51.1 to -48.3	-25 to -20	4b	-31.7 to -28.9	10 to 15	8a	-12.2 to -9.4
-55 to -50	1b	-48.3 to -45.6	-20 to -15	5a	-28.9 to -26.1	15 to 20	8b	-9.4 to -6.7
-50 to -45	2a	-45.6 to -42.8	-15 to -10	5b	-26.1 to -23.3	20 to 25	9a	-6.7 to -3.9
-45 to -40	2b	-42.8 to -40.0	-10 to -5	6a	-23.3 to -20.6	25 to 30	9b	-3.9 to -1.1
-40 to -35	3a	-40.0 to -37.2	-5 to 0	6b	-20.6 to -17.8			
-35 to -30	3b	-37.2 to -34.4	0 to 5	7a	-17.8 to -15.0			

From Natural Resources Canada website,
www.planthardiness.gc.ca

Index of Bird-Attracting Plants

When planning a bird-attracting backyard, a gardener has a vast range of trees, shrubs, and flowers from which to choose. Still, when making a selection, keep in mind that not every species is suitable for every area. For example, a lovely vine may be just right for the Southeast, but planted in the Pacific Northwest, it turns into an invasive weed. If you're not sure, check with a reliable nursery or the local USDA Cooperative State Extension Service to find out which species are problem-free. Also use the USDA Plant Hardiness Zone Map opposite. Most nurseries and seed catalogs list zone ranges for each plant, which tell you whether it's capable of growing in a geographic area, based mainly on its ability to withstand the minimum temperatures of the zone. *NOTE: Bold page numbers and botanical names in capital letters indicate featured plants. Gallery images not included.*

Photography Credits

The following abbreviations are used: BSP—*Big Stock Photo*; Fl—*Flickr*; FWS—*U.S. Fish and Wildlife Service*; iSP—*iStockphoto*; JI—*Jupiterimages*; SS—*Shutterstock*; USDA—*U.S. Department of Agriculture*; Wi—*Wikimedia*.

r = right; *l* = left; *m* = middle; *t* = top; *b* = bottom

FRONT COVER: SS/FotoRequest

BACK COVER: *tl* SS/Dhoxax *tml* SS/Chas *tmr* Fl/Brittney Bush *tr* SS/teekaygee *lmt* SS/Stubblefield Photography *lm* SS/pix2go *lmb* SS/Steven R. Hendricks *lb* Fl/Eric Brown

All "Favorite Food" photos JI, except acorns (SS/ Aleš Studený); berries (SS/UncleGenePhoto); flower (Wi/Michael Maggs); fly (isP/peaz); grasshopper (SS/Ravshan Mirzaitov); insect eggs (Wi/Flr0002); nuts (SS/Kaygorodov Yuriy); and worm (SS/Sue Robinson).

3*tl* SS/Steve Byland 4*tl* SS/Steve Byland 4*mr* Wi 4*br* Wi/Elaine R. Wilson 5*ml* SS/Tony Campbell 5*tr* SS/Gregg Williams 5*br* Wi/MDF 6 SS/Tony Campbell 7 SS/Joy Brown 8*tm* SS/ Stephanie Frey 8*bl* JI 9*tl* SS/Norman Pogson 9*br* SS/Masonjar 10*tl* SS/Hamíza Bakirci 10*b* SS/Loskutnikov 11 SS/Claud B. 12*tl* SS/Steve Byland 12*tr* SS/Dhoxax 12*b* SS/Robert A. Mansker 13*t* SS/Jill Lang 13*bl* SS/Mike Truchon 14 SS/Gilles DeCruyenaere 15 SS/Sebastian Knight 16*tl* SS/Peter Turner Photography 16*tr* SS/Baisa 16*bl* SS/Leene 16–17 SS/Blue Corner Studio 17*tl* SS/Reimar 17*br* SS/jaimie tuchman 18*m* SS/damann 18*tl* SS/Steve Byland 18*tr* Wi/MDF 18*bl* SS/Tony Campbell 19*m* SS/Vahan Abrahamyan 19*tl* SS/Doug Lemke 19*tr* SS/Jason Cheever 19*bl* SS/Steve Byland 20*m* SS/Chris Hill 20*tl* Wi/MDF 20*tr* SS/Arto Hakola 20*bl* SS/Steve Byland 21*m* SS/Krzysztof Slusarczyk 21*tl* SS/teekaygee 21*tr* SS/Steve Byland 21*bl* Alan D. Wilson, www.naturespicsonline.com 22*m* SS/ Alena A 22*tl* SS/Gregg Williams 22*tr* SS/John A. Anderson 22*bl* iSP/Frank Leung 23*m* SS/Evan Lorne 23*tl* SS/Jason Cheever 23*tr* SS/robag 23*bl* SS/Steve Byland 24*m* SS/atiger 24*tl* Steve Byland 24*tr* SS/Steve Byland 24*bl* SS/Chesapeake Images 25*m* SS/islavicek 25*tl* SS/Captain Tucker 25*bl* SS 26 SS/nipastock 26*tl* Fl/Blake Matheson 26*tr* SS/Wildlife 26*bl* Wi/Cephas 27*m* SS/LutsenkoLarissa 27*tl* Wi/ The Lilac-Breasted Roller 27*tr* SS/Robag 27*bl* SS/Paul Reeves Photography 28*m* SS/Lapis2380 28*tl* SS/Michael Woodruff 28*tr* SS/Steve Byland 28*bl* SS/N. Frey Photography 29*m* SS/ David Lingholm 29*tl* SS/Stubblefield Photography 29*tr* SS/ Paul Reeves Photography 29*bl* iSP/Paul Tessler 30*m* SS/ Darknessss 30*tl* SS/Michael Woodruff 30*tr* Fl/John Benson 30*bl* SS/Doug Lemke 31*m* SS/Victoria Tucholka 31*tl* SS/Cathy Keifer 31*tr* iSP/Mr Jamsey 31*bl* SS/Marcin Perkowski 32*m* SS/ Jacquie Klose 32*tl* SS/Jeff W. Jarrett 32*tr* Fl/Drew Weber 32*bl* FWS/David Brezinski 33*m* SS/Nick Pecker 33*tl* Wi/MDF 33*tr* SS/Chesapeake Images 33*bl* SS/Jason Cheever 34*m* SS/Ellen McKnight 34*tl* SS/Jason Cheever 34*tr* SS 34*bl* Wi/Elaine R. Wilson 35*m* SS/Milosz Maslanka 35*tl* SS/Steve Byland 35*tr* Wi/MDF 35*bl* SS/Steve Byland 36*m* SS/yanami 36*tl* SS/Bruce MacQueen 36*tr* SS/Cephas 36*bl* SS/Jim Nelson 37*m* SS/ Stephen B. Goodwin 37*tl* Wi/Will Sweet 37*tr* Wi/MDF 37*bl* SS/Cathy Keifer 38*m* SS/Miti74 38*tl* SS/Bryan Eastham 38*tr* SS/Cephas 38*bl* SS/Gregg Williams 39*m* SS/guentermanaus 39*tl* SS/Paul S. Wolf 39*tr* iSP/Noah Strycker 39*bl* SS/David Watkins 40*m* SS/Gerry Bishop 40*tl* SS/Steve Byland 40*tr* SS/ Mark Tegges 40*bl* FWS/David Brezinski 41*m* SS/Dewi Cahyaningrum 41*tl* Wi/Wolfgang Wander 41*tr* SS/Wildlife 41*bl* Fl/Blake Matheson 42*tl* SS 42*tr* SS/LorraineHudgins 42*bl* SS/Michael Woodruff 42*br* SS/Jim Nelson 43 *tl* SS/Michael Woodruff 43*ml* Wi/Joe Schneid 43*bl* Wi/Elaine R. Wilson 43*r* SS/Doug Lemke 44*ml* SS/Michael Woodruff 44*bl* Fl/Michael Shealy 44*mr* SS/Max Voran 45–1 SS/Chris Hill 45–2 Fl/Amy B 45–3 Fl/Boff_Hiroshi 45–4 USDA 45–5 Wi/Walter Siegmund 45*bl* SS/Christina Richards 46*ml* SS/Paul S. Wolf 46*mr* Fl/Eric Brown 46*bl* Wi/Tinodela 47–1 Wi/Sue in AZ 47–2 JI; 47–3 Wi 47–4 USDA 47*bl* SS/Todd Boland 48*ml* Wi/Cephas 48*mr* SS/ teekaygee 48*bl* FWS 49–1 USDA 49–2 SS/Mary Terriberry 49–3 SS/Sally Scott 49*ml* SS/Gail Johnson 49*bl* SS/teekaygee 50*ml* Wi/Wolfgang Wander 50*mr* SS/teekaygee 51–1 SS/Richard A. McGuirk 51–2 SS/efirm; 51–3 SS/ultimathule 51*bl* JI 52*ml* Fl/ Blake Matheson 52*mr* SS/Gregg Williams 52*bl* Fl/M. E.

Sanseverino 53–1 JI 53–2 SS/Norbert Rehm 53–3 SS/Natalie Erhova 53–4 Wi/Luis Fernández García 53*bm* SS/Bruce MacQueen 54-l SS/Mark Tegges 54*r* Fl/Henry T. McLin 55–1 SS/Suzanne Tucker 55–2 SS/Armin Rose 55–3 The Dow Gardens Archive, Dow Gardens, Bugwood.org 55–4 Wi/ EnLorax 55–*bl* JI 56*ml* SS/David Watkins 56–*r* Fl/Tim Lenz 56–*l* Fl/Mike Allen 57–1 SS/Mark Herreid 57–2 Jeff Peterson Xeriscape Garden, City of Loveland, Colorado 57–3 SS/ Weldon Schloneger 57–4 SS/Chris Hill 57–5 Wi/Ken Pei 57*bl* JI 58*ml* Alan D. Wilson, www.naturespicsonline.com 58*r* SS/ Norman Bateman 59–1 SS/jennyt 59–2 SS/Rob Byron 59–3 SS/ Serg Zastavkin 59*bl* Fl/Pat Anderson 60*ml* FSW/David Brezinski 60*mr* SS/Wildlife 60*bl* Fl/Henry McLin 61–1 Wi/ Ragesoss 61–2 Wi/Rasbak 61–3 Wi/SriMesh 61–4 Fl/jam343 61*bl* SS/Daniel E. Johnson 62*ml* Wi/Dominic Sherony 62*mr* SS/Daniel E. Johnson 62*bl* JI 63–1 SS/Doug Matthews 63–2 Wi/Stan Shebs 63–3 Wi/Rasbak 63–4 SS/Morten Kjerfulf 64*ml* iSP/Noah Strycker 64*bl* Fl/Joseph Oliver 65–1 Wi/Walter Siegmund 65–2 SS/Ken Schulze 65–3 Wi/Chhe 65–4 Wi/James K. Lindsey 65–5 Wi/Cory Maylett 65*bl* JI 66*ml* SS/Steve Byland 66*mr* SS/Arto Hakola 66*bl* Wi/bukk 67–1 SS/Jason Vandehey 67–2 SS/Chesapeake Images 67–3 SS/Kirsanov 67– 4 SS/Megan R. Hoover 67*bl* SS/Al Mueller 68*ml* SS/Wildlife 68*mr* Wi/The Lilac-Breasted Roller 68*bl* Wi/Jerry Friedman 69–1 SS/Civdis 69–2 SS/bierchen 69–3 SS/JC Hix 69–4 SS/ Doug Lemke 69*bl* SS/operative401 70*ml* SS/Marcin Perkowski 70*mr* Wi/Darren Swim 71–1 iSP/Robin Arnold 71–2 SS/David Máška 71–3 JI 71–4 JI 71*bl* SS/Bencha Stewart 72*ml* Wi/Elaine R. Wilson 72*mr* Wi/Elaine R. Wilson 73–1 Wi/Walter Siegmund 73–2 SS/Andrew Williams 73–3 SS/Jiri Slama 73*bl* SS 74*ml* SS/Steve Byland 74*mr* SS/Tony Campbell 74*bl* SS/Susan Law Cain 75–1 Wi/Bidgee 75–2 SS/Steve Byland 75–3 Wi/ Hardy Plants 75–4 Wi/VanHart 75*bl* Wi/Chris Alcock 76*ml* iSP/Mr Jamsey 76*mr* Fl/Brittney Bush 77–1 SS/Michael Solway 77–2 JI 77–3 JI 77*bl* SS/Norman Bateman 78*ml* SS/Bryan Eastham 78*mr* Fl/Henry T. McLin 78*bl* BSP/BVP 79–1 SS/ Bidouze Stéphane 79–2 SS/LesPalenik 79–3 FWS 79–4 FWS 79–5 SS/Sharon Day 79*bl* SS/Charlene Key 80*ml* SS/teekaygee 80*mr* teekaygee 81–1 Fl/Dogtooth77 81–2 SS/riekephotos 81–3 SS/Joy Stein 81–4 USDA 81*bl* SS/Jim Dubois 82*ml* SS/Bruce MacQueen 82*mr* SS/Gilles DeCruyenaere 83–1 Wi/Jaknouse 83–2 Wi/Jean-Pol Grandmot 83–3 SS/Todd Boland 83–4 SS/ Chris Hill 84*ml* SS/Chesapeake Images 84*mr* Fl/babyruthinmd 85–1 Wi/Neva Micheva 85–2 SS/LijuanGuo 85–3 SS/Yuguesh Fagoonee 85–4 Wi/B.navez 85*bl* SS/Norman Bateman 86*ml* SS/ robag 86*mr* SS/robag 86*bl* JI 87–1 SS/Bonnie Watton 87–2 SS/ Rodion 87–3 SS/NoniGlobalNetwork.com 87–4 Wi/SB Johnny 87*bl* SS/robag 88*ml* Wi/Captain-tucker 88*mr* SS/Chesapeake Images 88*bl* SS/Tony Campbell 89–1 Wi/Derek Ramsey 89–2 FWS 89–3 SS/Brykaylo Yuriy 89–4 USDA 89*bl* SS/Dennis Donohue 90*ml* iSP/Paul Tessler 90*mr* JI 90*bl* JI 91–1 SS/svehlik 91–2 Wi/Ben Cody 91–3 USDA 91*bl* Wi/Jerry Friedman 92*ml* SS/Frode Jacobsen 92*mr* FWS 93–1 SS/Dennis Donohue; 93–2 SS/Rafa Fabrykiewicz 93–3 SS/Chris Hill 93–4 Wi/Georg Slickers 94*ml* SS/Steve Byland 94*mr* Fl/Stuart Oikawa 95–1 SS/ Bonnie Watton 95–2 Wi/Forest & Kim Starr 95–3 SS/plampy 95–4 SS/USDA 95*bl* SS/Marcin Perkowski 96*ml* SS/Paul Reeves Photography 96*mr* SS/LorraineHudgins 96*bl* JI 97–1 SS/Tony Campbell 97–2 SS/Blanche Branton 97–3 Wi/Grandpa David 97–4 Wi/Sten Porse 98*ml* SS/Tony Campbell 98*mr* Wi/Derek Ramsey 99–1 Wi/Robert H. Mohlenbrock 99–2 BSP 99–3 USDA 99–4 Wi/MPF 99*bl* SS/Saforrest 100 SS 100*mr* Fl/ Randomtruth 100*bl* Fl/Randomtruth 101–1 Wi/Walter Siegmund 101–2 SS/Palych 101–3 SS/Christa DeRidder 101*bl* Fl/Jasper Nance 102*ml* SS/Jeff W. Jarrett 102*mr* SS/Hway Kiong Lim 102*bl* JI 103–1 Wi/Henryhartley 103–2 SS/Sharon Day 103–3 Wi/Jonathan Cardy 103–4 JI 103*bl* SS/Karel Brož 104*ml* SS/Chesapeake Images 104*mr* SS/Chesapeake Images 105–1 SS/Liga Lauzuma 105–2 JI 105–3 Fl/hickoryrose 105–4 JI 105–5 Wi/sarefo 105*bl* FWS 106*ml* SS/Stubblefield Photography 106*ml* SS/Steve Byland 106*bl* SS/Steve Byland 107–1 Wi/BotBln 107–2 Nature Nole 107–3 Wi/Markus Hagehlocher 107–4 WI/Wildfeuer 107*bl* Wi/Srobideau 108*ml* SS/Cathy Keifer 108*mr* SS/Stubblefield Photography 109–1 Wi/Brad Haire 109–2 SS/J. L. Levy 109–3 SS/Branka VV 109–4 JI 109*bl* Wi 110*ml* SS/Jason Cheever 110*mr* Wi/Walter

Siegmund 111–1 Fl/timmenzies 111–2 Wi/Sten Porse 111–3 Wi/ Velela 111–4 Wi/A. Barra 112*ml* Wi/Mdf 112*mr* Fl/Rick Leche 113–1 Wi/Charro Badger 113–2 Fl/C. V. Vick 113–3 Wi/Derek Ramsey 113–4 FWS 113*bl* Fl/Jonathan Brennecke 114*ml* SS/ Jason Cheever 114*mr* SS/Bruce MacQueen 114*bl* SS/Callahan Family Photography 115–1 Wi/Shawn Hanrahan 115–2 Wi/ Antilived 115–3 Wi/Nadiatalent 115–4 Wi/John Delano 115–5 Fl/Laurel Fan 115*bl* SS/Olga Utlyakova 116*ml* SS/Doug Lemke 116*mr* SS/Steve Byland 117–1 SS/Martin Muránsky 117–2 Wi/ Tim Ross 117–3 SS/giedrius_b 117–4 SS/Knumina 117*bl* SS/ operative401 118*ml* SS/Mircea Costina 118*mr* Wi/Dori 119–1 iSP/Susanne Hindle-Kher 119–2 Wi 119–3 Wi/Stan Shebs 119–4 JI 119*bl* Wi/Quadell 120*ml* iSP/Frank Leung 120*mr* Wi/ Scott Catron 120*bl* Wi/Walter Siegmund 121–1 Wi/Clinton Steeds 121–2 SS/basel101658 121–3 SS/hallam creations 121*bl* Fl/quinet; 122*ml* SS/Gregg Williams 122*mr* SS/Raymond Kasprzak 122*bl* JI 123–1 SS/Dennis Donohue 123–2 SS/ Trance- Drumer 123–3 SS/Blacqbook 123–4 SS/Dennis Donohue 123*bl* JI 124*ml* SS/Steve Byland 124*mr* SS/Chas 124*bl* Wi/Basil 125–1 JI 125–2 SS/Olga Lipatova 125–3 SS/Vladimir Petrov 125*bl* SS/Sten Porse 125*bl* SS/Chas 126*ml* SS/John A. Anderson 126*mr* SS/Tim Pleasant 127–1 Wi/SB Johnny 127–2 Wi/Meggar 127–3 FWS 127*bl* iSP/Joel Johndro 128*ml* Wi/ Cephas 128*mr* SS/Steve Byland 128*bl* JI 129–1 Wi/Cody Hough 129–2 SS/MarFot 129–3 JI 129–4 SS/Melinda Fawver 129*bl* JI 130*ml* Fl/Drew Weber 130*mr* SS/Chas 131–1 JI 131–2 SS/Beth Van Trees 131–3 JI 131*bl* SS/Bull's-Eye Arts 132*ml* SS/ Steve Byland 132*mr* iSP/Frank Leung 133–1 SS/Eduard Kyslynsky 133–2 JI 133–3 SS/Elena Moiseeva 133–4 Wi/Derek Ramsey 133*bl* SS/Melinda Fawver 134*ml* Wi/Cephas 134*mr* Wi/Cephas 134*bl* SS/Danno 3 135–1 Wi/Joaquim Alves Gaspar 135–2 SS/Kuskon 135–3 Wi/Jean-Pol Grandmont 135–4 JI 135*bl* Wi/Mary Terriberry 136*ml* SS/Jim Nelson 136*mr* SS/Chas 137–1 SS/Martin Novak 137–2 SS/Luca Villanova 137–3 SS/ Nikita Tiunov 137*bl* SS/Chris Alcock 138*ml* SS/N. Frey Photography 138*mr* SS/Steve Byland 139–1 Wi/Cephas 139–2 SS/Helder Almeida 139–3 SS/Brykaylo Yuriy 139*bl* SS/Gregory Johnston 140*ml* JI 140*mr* SS/Tony Campbell 141–1 SS/iofoto 141–2 SS/Kathrine Lloyd 141–3 SS/Shutterschock 141 *bl* Wi/ Mdf 142*ml* SS 142*mr* SS/Steven R. Hendricks 143–1 Wi/Ryan Berdeen 143–2 Wi/SriMesh 143–3 USDA 143–4 Wi/Tchacka 144*ml* Wi/Mdf 144*mr* Fl/D. L. Lindsey 145–1 Wi/Yan Simkin 145–2 SS/pjhpix 145–3 Wi/Derek Ramsey 145–4 SS/Luis Santos 146*ml* SS/Gregg Williams 146*mr* SS/pix2go 146*bl* SS/Bull's-Eye Arts 147–1 SS/Attl Tibor 147–2 SS/ER_09 147–3 SS 147–4 Wi/ Athantor 147*bl* SS/Melissa Dockstader 148*ml* SS/Arto Hakola 148*mr* SS/Michael Ledray 148*bl* SS/Ken Brown 149–1 SS/ Casey K. Bishop 149–2 SS/michael ledray 149–3 SS/Kathrine Lloyd 149–4 Wi/Calibas 149*bl* Wi/Matthew Field 150*ml* Wi/ Mdf 150*mr* Wi/Mdf 151–1 SS/SF Photo 151–2 SS/Philipe Ancheta 151–3 SS/Yanik Chauvin 151–4 Wi/Jerry Friedman 152*ml* SS/Steve Byland 152*mr* SS/Doug Lemke 152*bl* JI 153–1 Wi/Joe Schneid 153–2 SS/Jill Lang 153–3 SS/KellyNelson 153–4 SS/Chas 153*bl* JI 154*r* SS/Lana B 154*b* SS/Jeri Bland 155*t* from *Mid-Atlantic Home Landscaping, Third Edition*/Jerry Pavia 155*b* SS/Gyuszko-Photo 156*tl* SS/Kristi Blokhin 156*tr* SS/ Andriy Blokhin 156*b* SS/Artazum 157*t* from *Mid-Atlantic Home Landscaping, Third Edition*/Jerry Pavia 157*b* SS/Jamie Hooper 158 SS/Chiyacat 159*t* from *Mid-Atlantic Home Landscaping, Third Edition*/Jerry Pavia 159*b* from *Home Gardener's Small Gardens*/AG&G Books 160*t* SS/Svineyard 160*b* SS/Jorge Salcedo 161*t* from *California Home Landscaping, Third Edition*/Charles Mann 161*b* from *Home Gardener's Small Gardens*/David Squire 162*t* SS/Badon Hill Studio 162*b* SS/Lori Butcher 163*t* from *California Home Landscaping, Third Edition*/Charles Mann 163*b* from *Home Gardener's Wildlife Gardens*/AG&G Books 164 SS/fotocraft 165*t* from *California Home Landscaping, Third Edition*/Saxon Holt 165*b* from *Home Gardener's Wildlife Gardens*/AG&G Books 166*t* SS/Elena Elisseeva 166*b* SS/Pete Wise 167*t* from *Southeast Home Landscaping, Third Edition*/Jerry Pavia 167*b* from *Home Gardener's Wildlife Gardens*/John Freeman 168*t* SS/wheatley 168*b* SS/Elena Elisseeva 169*t* from *Mid-Atlantic Home Landscaping, Third Edition*/Jerry Pavia 169*b* SS/ Jamie Hooper